(Courtesy of Col. J.J. Campbell)

TURNER PUBLISHING COMPANY

Camp Lejeune, NC. Supply Bn, Norfolk, VA, in field during 2 week active duty. From left: Maj. Charles Jenkins; Maj. Hugh L. Dougherty, Jr.; General (unknown); Lt. Col. Walter Galiford; Officer (unknown). Mid 1970s. (Courtesy of H.L. Dougherty.)

TURNER PUBLISHING COMPANY

Copyright © 2000 Marine Corps Reserve Officers' Association
Publishing Rights: Turner Publishing Company
This book or any part thereof may not be reproduced without the
written consent of MCROA and the publisher.

Turner Publishing Company Staff:
Randy Baumgardner, Editor
Shelley R. Davidson, Designer

Library of Congress Catalog Card Number 98-89381

ISBN: 978-1-63026-964-7

Additional copies may be purchased directly
from the publisher. Limited Edition.

4

TABLE OF CONTENTS

INTRODUCTION

The Marine Corps Reserve Officers' Association is pleased to participate with the Turner Publishing Company in the publication of this book about our history. We wish to thank all of those members who submitted their biographies and photographs and then waited patiently for it to be published.

As MCROA enters the 21st century, it does so with the same philosophy and objectives that were created by its founding father's 74 years ago:

<u>Our philosophy is:</u> " **to at all times retain an independent voice as to when and how to best assist the Marine Corps."**

<u>Our objectives have always been</u>: **"to foster the advancement of the professional and technical skills of reserve officers; to promote the interest of reserve officers in the United States Marine Corps and the interest of the United States Marine Corps in reserve officers; to represent and assist individual members; and, at all times to promote the interests of the United States Marine Corps in the broadest and most liberal manner to the end that it may best advance the welfare of and serve to preserve the security of the United States."**

<u>Our slogan is</u>: **"There will always be a United States as long as there is a United States Marine Corps, and there will always be a United States Marine Corps as long as there is a United States Marine Corps Reserve and, there will always be a United States Marine Corps Reserve as long as there is a United States Marine Corps Reserve Officers Association."**

We would like to thank the following individuals who helped gather information, experiences and photographs, and assisted in the administrative tasks that resulted in this book becoming a reality.

- Ms. Yana Ginsberg, Center of Naval Analysis and former writer for the Navy Times, and
- GySgt Tom Green, USMC (Ret), MCROA's executive assistant for the last 10 years

HISTORY

*1st Marine Corps District Reserve
Conference, New Yorker Hotel, 1965.
(Courtesy of Col. J.J. Campbell)*

Introduction—73 Years of Service to the Corps

Minutes before the sun rose over the sweeping desert landscape that stretches between Saudi Arabia and Kuwait the Marines of Bravo Company, 4th Tank Battalion heard an unwelcome but all too familiar sound—enemy tanks. Only weeks before these Marines had been called up from their civilian lives to leave their homes and jobs and serve. By the end of that February day the Marines of Bravo Company, a unit out of Yakima, Washington, had obliterated 34 out of 35 enemy tanks without suffering a single casualty.

The skill and courage of these Marines would become one of the most famous stories of Marine performance in the Gulf War.

In November 1990, President George Bush called up 200,000 troops to reinforce the US Central Command as the United States prepared for a confrontation with Iraqi president Saddam Hussein. Reservists from all branches of service were called. Among them were 80 units of the Selected Marine Corps Reserve. It has become conventional wisdom that without the Reserve the nation's military could not have gone to war, much less been so spectacularly successful. During Operations Desert Shield and Desert Storm over 31,000 Marine Corps reservists were mobilized and more than 13,000 were deployed to the war.[1]

When the United States first made the decision to commit forces to cut short Saddam Hussein's ambitions, Marine Corps leadership did not want to call out the Reserves for at least 60 days. It was a long-standing Marine Corps policy to be able to deploy and sustain a force for nearly two months before calling in reinforcements. However, by the fall of 1990 the Corps was already fully committed and there was little choice but to activate Reserve units to join the fight.

By the end of the war General Colin Powell would state that "We could not have gone to war without them [the Reserves], and they were to perform superbly."

Eight decades ago it would have been almost impossible to foresee Marine Corps reservists capable of coming together in some coherent fashion, much less being able to successfully fight alongside their active duty brethren on a dusty desert battlefield in the Middle East. But one man believed that the Reserve in particular and the Marine Corps in general would be a fighting force of distinction as long as Marines received the right training, equipment and support.

Seventy-three years ago, a young Marine realized that battlefield glory alone would not secure the Corps' place among the nation's service branches. The nation's leadership and citizens would have to be reminded of the value Marines provided to the national defense not only during war, but during peacetime as well. That man, the formidable Melvin J. Maas, would turn that belief into an organization that has fought and argued on behalf of all Marines for more than seventy years.

Over the last seven decades the focus of MCROA has shifted from legislation to chapter longevity. During each successive decade MCROA has sought to help Marine Corps Reservists and the whole Marine Corps. Whether in front of a congressional committee discussing key pieces of legislation, or at work behind the scenes in the halls of Headquarters Marine Corps, MCROA has always aimed at being an advocate that was in the right place at the right time.

During the 20s, MCROA, as well as the Marine Corps Reserve, was in its infancy. These early years would be spent building the neophyte organizations.

In the 30s, MCROA would join with the Corps to help define its mission and argue for the Corps' value to the nation's overall defense structure.

As World War II broke out across Europe, eventually reaching US shores in 1941, MCROA would put the Corps and the call to duty ahead of its own development. However, the post war years would keep the members of MCROA so busy that it would seem like its activities had hardly been suspended during the war effort.

In the late 40s and 50s MCROA would enter its golden age of political activism. As the Corps once again battled for its survival, MCROA's influence and voice would prove invaluable not only to the Reserve Forces but to the Corps as a whole.

A change in focus was in store starting with the 60s. MCROA's political activism would diminish as the association turned its gaze inward and started to emphasize professional development for its membership, the growth and strengthening of the organization, and community outreach. It would also be a decade of disappointment, as for the first time in American history the Reserves would not be called up as a fighting force for a major US war.

In the aftermath of Vietnam, MCROA and the Reserves would have to battle a tarnished image. The decade would witness a growing rift between the military and the American public. Tensions also flared within the military as drugs, race-relations and a proposed end of the draft made the decade a bumpy one indeed. Additionally, topics such as recruitment, training and equipment–although perennial issues–would gain importance as defense budgets shrank and the Reserves were increasingly perceived as underused, "weekend warriors."

During the 80s, equity would be MCROA's goal. Although defense spending would climb to an all time high in the nation's history, the Reserves faced equipment and funding shortages that would not be remedied for another decade.

Many, including MCROA, saw the Reserve contribution to the Gulf War effort as a vindication for the many battles for funding, integrated training and modern equipment. Based on reservists' performance and further downsizing of the military, members of USMCR have become increasingly sought after to perform missions, usually on extended active duty. Although the operational tempo of Marine reservists has meant fewer are able to actively participate in MCROA, the association can take credit for the place the Marine Corps has come to hold in the overall Corps.

THE 1920s—IN THE BEGINNING[2]

It is important to understand the context within which MCROA came into being. To begin with, no Marine Corps Reserve existed officially until President Wilson affixed his signature to the Act of 29 August 1916. Prior to this, however, the first Marine Corps Reserve unit in our nation's history actually was formed without legislative authority in November 1914, when the Massachusetts Naval Militia formed the 1st Marine Company.

Unofficially, there was always a Marine Corps component imbedded within the state controlled Naval Militias in the late 1800s and early 1900s. The road to a federal reserve program began in 1900 when it became clear that state run militias could not properly provide for a second line of defense in case of a national emergency. The problem was getting control of the Naval Reserve away from the states. It was a political battle and the Navy finally created a Division of Naval Militia Affairs in the Navy Department in 1914. The following year the Navy issued a follow-on order specifically creating a Marine Corps Branch within the naval militia.

On 6 April 1917, when World War I was declared, the Reserve was composed of three officers and 33 enlisted men. At the close of World War I, it consisted of 276 officers and 5,968 enlisted men. During the course of the war, all who entered the Marine Corps for the "duration" were reserves but were on definite term enlistments or appointments which expired at the end of the war, and little effort was made to encourage re-enrollments. At the conclusion of World War I these men either became members of the regular establishment or returned to civilian life.

During the 1920s one of the great political movements in this country was an effort to achieve disarmament and a reduction of armed forces. This brought about an even more pronounced withdrawal by the then War and Navy departments from any legislative efforts, which might have affected the maintenance of our rapidly diminishing regular establishments. Nevertheless, the Naval Reserve Act of 1925 was passed and became effective on 1 July 1925, authorizing the creation of a Marine Corps Reserve and providing for the first time for drill and annual training duty pay.

At the same time a young man named Melvin Maas gathered a group of young officers in Washington DC to discuss the state of the Reserve and its future. Maas had served as an enlisted man in World War I and had received his commission as a first lieutenant during the same time that the Naval Reserve Act of 1925 was passed. Knowing first hand the training inadequacies of the Reserve and recognizing the need for a strong and thriving Marine Corps and Marine Corps Reserve, the group of young officers planted the seeds of what eventually would grow into the Marine Corps Reserve Officers Association.

It was decided that MCROA would focus on building a strong Reserve component by being an advocate of the Marine Corps—voicing its views before the Congress of the United States and in the halls of the Navy and War Departments and at the White House. Maas and his group of officers recognized from the beginning that a strong reserve could only exist through a strong regular establishment, which made it a primary objective of MCROA to support fully the regular as well as the reserve components to the fullest extent possible. Their philosophy became the opening words of the MCROA charter:

"To foster the advancement of the professional and technical skills of reserve officers; to promote the interest of reserve officers in the United States Marine Corps and the interest of the United States Marine Corps in reserve officers; to represent and assist individual members; and, at all times to promote the interests of the United States Marine Corps in the broadest and most liberal manner to the end that it may best advance the welfare of and serve to preserve the security of the United States."

And so, on 10 November 1926, the 151st birthday of the Marine Corps, the Marine Corps Reserve Officers Association was officially born.

In 1926, the few reserve units that existed operated on an austerity basis. There was no formal training program in place and hardly any funds available to the newly formed Reserve component for training, site rentals, equipment or uniforms. The Reserve did the best it could, using rent-free facilities when they could be obtained to conduct training. Condemned buildings, Naval Militia armories, old barracks and the like were used as initial training sites. Funds for clothing and equipment were so limited that only a portion of the Reserve units could be supplied, the remainder being furnished only partial uniforms. There were no provisions for promotion, retirement or other benefits, which most Marine reservists have come to accept as givens of their reserve service.

In 1926, Melvin Maas was also elected to Congress as a representative from Minnesota. This event had a profound impact on the relationship MCROA would have with the Marine Corps and Congress. Because of Maas' position and his leadership, the association gained an entree into both the halls of the Capitol and at Headquarters Marine Corps that later enabled MCROA to accomplish a great deal in the 40s and 50s.

From the outset the organization made its views known to the Commandant of the Marine Corps concerning the creation of a training program and the establishment of a promotion system consistent with the running mate system. The association also urged that there be reserve representation on the Marine Corps Policy Board, which had been established in 1925 but consisted only of active duty senior officers.

By 1928, Maas, as president of MCROA, was allowed to sit in on the Marine Corps Reserve Policy Board meetings. Eventually, reserve officers would come to serve on the board as voting members, rotating membership every two years. For many years there was a close relationship between the policy board and MCROA, since many of the officers who served on the board were also MCROA members. The relationship allowed issues to "trickle" up from SMCR units to the attention of local MCROA chapters, to the national headquarters and eventually to the policy board, where they then could be discussed and either passed on or turned into policy recommendations.

In 1929, MCROA would be successful in accomplishing a second objective. That year the first Marine Corps Reserve officer training camp was held at Quantico, Virginia. The two-week camp was a no pay affair, but according to reports published in the *Marine Corps Gazette*, the training was useful and the turnout good.

THE 1930S—FLIGHT AND FIGHT

In the decades leading up to World War II, the Reserves and MCROA were so intertwined that it was almost impossible to draw a line between the two. In fact, the early history of the reserves was in essence the early history of MCROA. This was especially true during the 30s when both groups were rapidly developing.

At the start of the decade however, it seemed that the Marine Corps' development would be stunted.

In 1930 President Hoover, as a cost-cutting measure, proposed merging the Marine Corps with the Army. Maas, who was not only MCROA's president but a congress-

man as well, got involved right away. In his capacity as the president of MCROA he took to the airwaves over an 87-station hookup with an appeal to the American public. Funds raised by fellow MCROA members helped Maas reach out across the airwaves. The result was an outpouring of more than 10,000 telegrams to President Hoover, urging him not to dissolve the Corps. Hoover agreed, however, he stipulated that the total strength of the Marine Corps not exceed 10,000.

Although the Marine Corps—active and reservist—was saved, this would not be the last time the nation's leaders would consider the possible dissolution of the USMC. Luckily, MCROA remained ever vigilant and made sure that the Corps would remain strong for years to come.

With the future of the Marine Corps secure, at least for the moment, the Reserve program continued to develop despite lean fiscal times.

Reserve aviation soared in the 30s.

Although a Reserve Air Corps was created in 1916, the Marine Corps had difficulty finding Marines interested in flying. After the Armistice the Reserve Flying Corps was almost eliminated due to demobilization. When the war ended many reserve pilots did not continue their aviation career in the Corps, instead choosing to finish out their enrollment period and return to civilian life. By March 1919, there were only 74 reserve pilots left on the Reserve Flying Corps' rolls.

The Reserve Act of 1925 established actual aviation units within the Reserve, but there was some initial friction between reservists and regulars who were both trying to train on the same, limited number of planes. The funding crunch was slightly alleviated in 1929 when Congress appropriated funds specifically for flight training. In 1930, Maas helped found the first Marine Aviation Squadron on a non-pay basis in Minneapolis.

Meanwhile, back on the ground Reservists were feeling the pinch.

In 1931, no funds were appropriated for drill pay, and had it not been for the loyal few who remained in the Reserve and attended drill at their own expense, without pay, the Reserve would have disappeared entirely. Fortunately, most units remained intact. In 1934, after the country had begun to recover from the economic blows of the Great Depression, drill pay was once again restored. However, the amount of funding available for drill pay was still severely limited and only a small percentage of the unit would receive any compensation. In true Marine Corps fashion, those Marines lucky enough to be paid would often share what money they received with their unpaid brothers.

At the time there was still no funding available for uniforms or shoes. Oftentimes the commanding officer of a unit would purchase shoes for his troops as a tool of recruitment. This state of affairs continued until the passage of the Naval Reserve Act of 1938.

The Naval Reserve Act of 1938 would be the first of many reorganization efforts affecting the Reserve. The 1938 legislation, passed on June 25th, made the Marine Corps Reserve a part of the Marine Corps as opposed to part of the Navy. It also provided for increased pay, an honorary retired list and three new reserve categories including the Fleet Marine Corps Reserve, the Organized Marine Corps Reserve and the Volunteer Marine Corps Reserve. This act, strongly supported by MCROA, would become the bedrock for all future Reserve legislation.[3]

THE 1940s—WAR DELAYS DEVELOPMENT

It seemed that just as the Marine Corps Reserve Officers Association got off the ground, its development was interrupted by the storm brewing across the ocean.

For the United States, World War II didn't officially start until 7 December 1941, when the Japanese launched a surprise attack against Pearl Harbor and the Pacific Fleet. But for the rest of the world the winds of war had started blowing as early as 1937, when Japan invaded China. At the time the United States was hardly prepared for war. Looking inward, not outward was the preferred foreign policy of the day. In 1935, after Italy invaded Ethiopia, an opinion poll asked Americans whether the United States should join with other nations to stop one nation from attacking another. No, said 67 percent of the respondents.[4]

America's military forces were equally as unprepared for war as the rest of the American public. After World War I, the country was weary of the terrible toll trench warfare had taken on troops and national resources. The nation, wishing to return to a more peaceful lifestyle, did not want a large military. Not only were there economic considerations, but also psychological ones for deflating military might. Having a large military only served to remind Americans of the tragic and horrible ordeal they and their allies had suffered "over there," even though they emerged victorious.

So in 1941, when the United States could no longer ignore the call to arms, the country was woefully unprepared and undermanned. At that time the regular Marine Corps only had an authorized strength of 45,000 men and two operational divisions.[5] Upon its creation in 1942, the 3rd Marine Division was immediately committed to combat in the Solomon Islands. A Reserve call–up became inevitable if the Marine Corps was to execute its wartime mission. In October 1940, President Franklin Roosevelt issued the call–up order. The first to mobilize were the 23 organized Reserve battalions. In November the Reserve aviation squadrons followed. Eventually the Reserves would account for 68 percent of the total Marine Corps fighting strength during World War II. But for all the bravery, glory and dedication the Reservists brought to the war effort, the call–up spelled the temporary end of MCROA.

Many of MCROA's leading officers were themselves recalled to the service of their country. Even the president, Melvin J. Maas, returned to sea to serve on the staffs of Admiral William Halsey and Admiral Frank J. Fletcher. Practically speaking, there was no one to attend to the administrative duties of running the association. So in 1940, the formal activities of MCROA were suspended. The association was placed in trusteeship, under the president, with the authority to reactivate after the war.[6]

By the end of the decade however, it would seem like MCROA had hardly taken a break at all. After hostilities ended in 1945, MCROA went into overdrive. Not only was there an association to rebuild, but the very existence of the Marine Corps was being threatened.

Rebuilding the association required leadership, a strong membership base and building. Initially, MCROA would have little time to attend to any of these matters. Demobilization, which started immediately, meant thousands of men and women were coming off active duty. Many wanted to retain their affiliation with the Corps in some manner. Marines turned to MCROA.

MCROA, happily, could barely keep up.

In the April 1946 newsletter MCROA informed its membership that "the volume of mail has made it impossible to answer all your letters individually. The Association started its reactivation in a very modest way but the response was so immediate that we could not build a headquarters organization fast enough to even begin to keep up with the rapidity of the increase in membership."[7]

The following month MCROA began chartering local chapters. National dues were $3.00. A minimum of 15 members was required. Chapters were usually named after famous Marines or battles involving the Corps. Initially the chapters' goals were practical. Most Marines joined local chapters to keep abreast of important policy developments and other USMC related news. The national headquarters also encouraged chapters to help members in their transition back into civilian life by aiding in job searches for both officers and enlisted Marines.

Some, however, simply missed the camaraderie they had come to know and value while they were on active duty.

"I look forward with much interest to the organization's future activities and developments. Since reverting to an inactive status, I have missed very much the routine, friendships, and developments in the Corps, and sincerely hope I can reestablish a closer contact with the Corps as a member of MCROA," wrote one member in a letter to the association, in the spring of 1946.

While the association got itself internally organized, MCROA's legislative task list grew almost overnight.

National president and founder Melvin Maas appeared before the House Armed Services Committee in 1947 in support of the Reserve Retirement Bill, which would allow Reserve officers to earn a retirement after 20 years of satisfactory service. "The bill," argued Maas, "would in a very small way partially compensate reservists after long years of service in the Reserve, for their expenses and their economic loss which they have suffered by reason of their reserve activities."

During that same year, Maas, once again representing MCROA, appeared before Congress arguing against President Truman's proposed Unification Bill that would essentially have eliminated the Marine Corps entirely and folded the Corps into one overarching military department. Thanks in part to MCROA's efforts, the Marine Corps was spared. Instead, Congress passed the National Security Act of 1947 which established the Department of Defense, the Joint Chiefs of Staff and made the Secretary of Defense a cabinet level position. The act also established three separate service departments, making the Marine Corps a part of the Department of Navy.

Off of Capitol Hill, MCROA focused on issues closer to home.

In the spring of 1948, MCROA held its first post-war national conference. The one day affair was a far cry from the modern MCROA military conference, but it was something MCROA members had anxiously been lobbying the national leadership for.

Held in Washington, 29 May, the conference was aimed at chapter presidents rather than the general membership. The conference program featured Vice Admiral A.W. Radford, the Vice-Chief of Naval Operations and Major General W.T. Clement, Marine Corps Reserve Director. Also featured was a special panel of defense writers to discuss the "Future of the Marine Corps."

MCROA's annual conference would be held in the spring of every year, from that point forward and until the mid-1950s, in the nation's capitol, Washington DC.

THE 1950s—TWO WARS AND A REORGANIZATION

The North Korean People's Army surprised South Korea and the rest of the world when it invaded its southern neighbor on 25 June 1950. In the first Cold War confrontation the Marine Corps and the Marine Corps Reserve proved themselves not only willing, but also incredibly able in their struggle against "Communist aggression."

On 19 July 1950, the "Minute Men" of the Organized Reserve were mobilized for active duty. Approximately 21,000 reservists were ordered to Camp Pendleton, California and another 5,800 to Camp Lejeune, North Carolina.

Over 90 percent of reserve officers and enlisted men reported for duty in Korea. When war erupted in the summer of 1950, 1st Marine Division was severely undermanned at 3,386 officers and men of the 20,000 that were needed to complete the landing at Inchon. Building up manpower through the draft was impractical because the Marine Corps needed combat ready men right away and the Reserve was the only logical choice.

At the time of the Inchon–Seoul operations, 15 September to 7 October 1950, there were more Marines in the Far East than there had been in the total Fleet Marine Force two and a half months earlier. Twenty percent of these were reservists only, six to eight weeks removed from their normal civilian lives.[8]

Although Marine reservists performed ably during the Korean conflict, the mobilization was not without its share of problems. The issues raised by the Korea call–up eventually led to multiple pieces of legislation that sought to improve training, mobilization processes and reserve manning. Once again, in the late 50s MCROA was active in helping build support for and seeking passage of new Reserve laws.

The Universal Military Training and Service Act of 1951 reaffirmed the principal of universal military obligation for all young men. The Armed Forces Reserve Act of 1952 required each service to commit to a program establishing strong reserve forces, more realistic training and expanded numbers. The new act obligated new members of the military to a combined eight-year commitment of active and reserve participation.[9]

The Reserve Officer Personnel Act was enacted into law on 3 September 1954. It provided for officer promotions, precedence, constructive credit, distribution and retention. One of the provisions required reservists to maintain a minimum of 27 retirement points in order to remain on "active status." Other provisions allowed for five Marine Corps Reserve general officers and required promotion board meetings to consider reserve officers for advancement, to be composed of at least 50 percent reserve members.[10]

The association's support of these reserve-related regulations were considered one of MCROA's greatest contributions on behalf of the Marine Corps Reserve, according to an earlier version of MCROA's history.

"In all probability the greatest direct contribution made by MCROA to Marine Reserve Officers in addition to assisting in the passage of Public Law 819 immediately after World War II was the powerful part played in the support of the passage of the Armed Forces Reserve Act of 1952 and the Reserve Officer Personnel Act of 1954 with subsequent amendments to both. General Maas wrote the provisions of these acts in consultation with the Armed Forces Reserve Policy Board, the officers of ROA and the Executive Council of MCROA."[11]

MCROA, however, was not so supportive of every piece of legislation that dealt with the Marine Corps and its Reserve. From 1949 until 1952 MCROA would engage in some bitter battles with Congress and the Truman Administration over the future of the Marine Corps. The debate about the future of the Corps would become one of MCROA's most famous moments.

Immediately after World War II there was talk of merging all of the services together to create one Department of Defense under the leadership of a single secretary. The merger efforts were blocked and the National Security Act of 1947 established the three service departments, four service branches, a Secretary of Defense and the Joint Chiefs of Staff. The legislation however did not establish, by statute, a floor for Marine Corps strength nor was the Commandant a member of the JCS.

As the fighting progressed in Korea and the Marine Corps continued to expand, Rep. Carl Vinson, one of the Corps biggest congressional supporters and chairman of the House Armed Services Committee, announced that he was in favor of a Marine Corps of four divisions and four wings.[12]

The idea was met with opposition from seemingly every corner. Neither the Department of Defense, the JCS, the Army, the Navy, nor the Truman Administration got behind the proposition.

But what really got the Marine Corps and its supporters up in arms was a letter Truman sent to Rep. Gordon McDonough calling the Marine Corps the Navy's police force. He also said in the letter that he didn't see anything wrong with the way things were.

The White House drew a hostile response from citizens, congressional supporters of the Corps and, most notably, MCROA. Seizing the opportunity, the firestorm of public opinion presented by Senator Paul Douglas (himself a member of MCROA), Vinson and Rep. Mike Mansfield urged the expansion of the Marine Corps and the addition of the Commandant as a full member of the JCS.

At the 1950 MCROA conference Maas, in his keynote address, tried to reassure delegates about the future.

"The movement to abolish or whittle away the Marine Corps has failed. We have been assured by no less than our commander in chief, President Truman and Secretary of Defense Louis Johnson that an effective, adequate Marine Corps will be maintained as an integral part of the United States Armed Forces," Maas told MCROA members. But members knew that legislation was better than promises. As a result of the 32 resolutions passed at the convention that year one called for making the CMC a member of the JCS and another called for establishing a personnel floor for the Corps.

Douglas, who was a speaker at the convention, introduced Senate Bill 677 in September 1950, which proposed a Marine Corps composed of four division and four wings, full membership on the JCS for the CMC and an assistant secretary of the Navy to represent Marine Corps interests. However, the bill would not be heard until the 82nd Congress convened in 1951. But even then the fight would drag on. In the House a similar version of the Douglas bill was a victim of roadblock after roadblock. By the spring of 1951, a version of each bill had been passed by both the House and the Senate. But neither chamber could reach a compromise. Although some headway had been made with regard to Corps manning and structure, the CMC's membership on the JCS was still a sticking point. Finally, that summer an agreement was struck. The Marine Corps would consist of at least three division and three air wings and the Commandant could sit on the JCS on all issues pertaining to the Corps. The Commandant would not become a full member of the JCS until 1978.

In the early 1950s, MCROA also faced some major turning points internally.

Maas, after serving as MCROA's founder, leader and president for a quarter of a century, finally stepped down as the head of MCROA due to blindness and failing health. In his final presidential speech at the 1951 convention, Maas summed up his MCROA career in the following words:

"I hand this challenge and this responsibility on to those who shall be selected today to carry on the direction of MCROA. As I say goodbye to you as your president, I wish to paraphrase a recent farewell of a great American. Old Marines, unlike soldiers, do not die; we don't fade away; we only step a pace to the rear. So as an old Marine, I do not fade away from you but only step back. I shall always be in there backing up younger Marines in the common job of preserving these magnificent United States, by always having a loyal fighting US Marine Corps to lead the task force in our preservation."

Colonel Justice M. Chambers succeeded Maas as the second national president of MCROA.

Not the least of MCROA's problems at the outbreak of the Korean War were the association's efforts to build up a strong chapter organization country–wide. However, those hopes were shattered as a result of the Reserve call–up. MCROA had used the Organized Reserve units around the country as a focal point for its chapter organization. At the onset of Korea, MCROA was left with only a skeleton organization. The rest of the reservists had gone off to war.

The 1960s—Building a Better MCROA

As reservists returned home from Korea and got back to "normal" life, MCROA began to tackle its internal affairs. Membership and chapter growth became more important than the legislative activism that marked the first three decades of MCROA's existence.

The 1960 MCROA Military Conference and Convention met in Chicago. A total of 350 MCROA members attended the weekend in the Windy City, but the conference was relatively lightweight. Members essentially reiterated their support of the Corps and the Eisenhower Administration and pledged to do their part in safeguarding the nation against the "Red Peril." The one substantive resolution to come out of the conference was a request for the Division of Reserve to review the officer manning levels and rank distribution policies in order to increase the number of field grade officers and senior captains authorized to participate in the Organized Reserve Program.

Later that spring, on 26 May 1960, MCROA's judge advocate, Col. Arthur Hanson, carried MCROA's message to the Senate Armed Services Committee, who was considering amendments to the Reserve Officers Promotion Act. Both Headquarters Marine Corps and the Department of the Navy had recommended that the Reserve officers be reduced from strength of 29,500 to 24,500. Because the number of officers eligible for promotion was based on a percentage of actual strength, MCROA's principal objection to the proposed cuts were the effect the downsizing would have on the number of officers who could be promoted.

By August 1960, Congress returned its decision.

The Reserve lost 5,000 men despite MCROA's argument to the contrary. However, Congress did change the way officers in the Reserve would be promoted from that point forward. Instead of basing a percentage of promotions on actual on-hand strength, promotion percentages would now be based on authorized strength.

Over the course of the next eight years the size and success of the MCROA annual military conference would grow. In 1967, conference attendance reached an all-time high of 800 officers and guests at the 41st annual conference held in Anaheim, Calif.

In the early 60s, the conventions were little more than run-downs of national headquarters' administrative matters and social events. But by 1968, the conventions became a forum for Marine Corps issues of the day, as well as opportunities for professional development for those who attended.

For example in 1965, as 3,000 Marines were landing in the Republic of Vietnam, some 500 MCROA members gathered in Washington, DC for the 39th MCROA con-

1st Marine Corps District Reserve Conference, 1964, Garden City, New York.

vention. Highlights of the convention included breakout sessions on the future of the US space program, Marine helicopter operations in Vietnam and developments in Marine gear.

"I, frankly, was never much of joiner," wrote one officer after being a MCROA member for two years. "I did not immediately join MCROA because I instinctively thought of it as just another social organization. After I did join, I attended a national conference and was most impressed with the leadership, fairness and objectivity with which major issues were discussed. I want you to know that I am and always will be proud to be a member of the Association."

During the latter half of the decade the conventions were used by MCROA and Marine Corps Reserve leadership as a podium from which to focus the efforts of local chapters, especially as the war in Vietnam escalated and public support of the war effort began to lag.

Speaking at the 39th annual conference, BGen. Joseph L. Stewart, Director Marine Corps Reserve told MCROA members that reservists would be most helpful to their fellow Marines overseas if they were:
- Knowledgeable about Corps and Reserve programs.
- Vocal about telling the Marine Corps and the Marine Corps Reserve story.
- Supportive of young officers' and NCOs' participation in the Reserves.

Increasing membership was also a key issue for MCROA in the 60s.

Although a healthy and active membership base was also a MCROA tenet, starting in 1963, there was renewed emphasis placed on recruiting fresh members.

"Every Reserve Officer Should Join MCROA," read the front page of the April 1963 issue of *The Word*. "To properly operate MCROA we need a minimum of 4,000 members. To do the job as it should be done we should have a membership of 6,500," stated the accompanying article.

In the fall MCROA launched a major membership drive, which was announced in the September 1963 issue of *The Word*. MCROA used the kick off to remind members and potential members alike of what the association had accomplished on their behalf over the years.

"Through the efforts of MCROA, the Organized Reserve, both ground and air, in its present state, has been made possible. Likewise the Volunteer Training program is the result of MCROA's insistence that a training program be provided for Reserve Officers who are not in organized units.

Public Law 810, which provides for the present Reserve Retirement benefits was passed and signed into law in 1948. This is the only legislative act ever written which provides longevity retirement pay for Reserve Officers.

Whatever Reserve activity you are in—Ready Reserve, Stand-by Reserve or Retired Reserve—MCROA has had a hand in making your participation possible. It is as little as you can do to support the organization that had made it all possible," read the printed plea for new blood.

At the 1964 conference MCROA Executive Chairman of the Board of Directors, Colonel Douglas Preacher stressed that "in times of quiet on the legislative front, the principal concern and effort...should be pointed toward increasing MCROA membership."

Unfortunately, the association never managed to crack the 6,500 figure it felt was so important to its own sustainment. For the duration of the decade MCROA's membership numbers would hover at approximately 4,500 members.

Membership, however, was not MCROA's only concern during the turbulent 1960s.

By the late 60s America's military was fully engaged in the jungles of Vietnam. However, for the first time in history, the Reserve was not called up to support a major war effort. Although most Marine Corps officers were reservists[13], no Organized Reserve units were deployed.

Instead, the Reserve and MCROA adopted a mission closer to home.

Late in 1965, the Reserves launched a new effort on behalf of the people of Vietnam—the Marine Corps Reserve Civic Action Program. This project gave each Marine reservist a direct and personal means of supporting United States efforts in Vietnam. Additionally, it afforded an excellent means of placing the Marine Corps and its Reserve before the public in a favorable light.

The fund was nationally authorized and locally implemented and was designed to assist the Regular forces who already were helping the poor in Vietnam through the donation of personal services, funds, and supplies.

"Inasmuch as the Commandant does not plan to ask that the Reserve be called to active duty before a specific mission exists, it is considered that the conduct of a joint Marine Reserve/CARE program is a task short of mobilization for which the Reserve is singularly qualified," read the order announcing the program.

MCROA immediately pushed its membership to help with fundraising for the new program. In its October 1965 newsletter the association asked members to "open your checkbook and send a check...to back up the tremendous job our Marines are doing in Vietnam."

In 1967, MCROA national president, Brigadier General Russell A. Bowen, traveled to Vietnam to see first hand how the program, which had topped $100,000 by August of that year, was working out.

"We must continue our efforts to increase the funds available for this important work. Though there is no substitute for a complete military victory, it is just as important that we win the hearts and minds of the South Vietnamese people, if we are to win peace as well," Bowen wrote in the September issue of *The Word*.

On a more personal note, all of MCROA suffered a great loss during the spring of 1964.

On 13 April 1964 General Melvin J. Maas passed away after a lengthy illness.

1st LT G.F. Merna enjoying a good meal, 3rd Marine Division, Vietnam, 1967.

"No one person in the history of our country has ever devoted himself more selflessly to his nation and the people of his country than did Mel Maas. Without fear, he faced up to many, many crises in legislation and in war, which would have turned lesser men's heads aside.

Mel Maas is more responsible for the creation of the reserve forces of this nation that saved this country from defeat in World War II than any other American," read the eulogy offered by *The Word*. "May God rest his soul. May we inherit a touch of his courage to carry on the work with which he ennobled his fellow countrymen."

THE 1970's—AFTER VIETNAM

Outreach at the local level became MCROA's core competency in the post-Vietnam era. Sweeping policy changes, returning war veterans, and a recruiting crunch made MCROAns' role as bridge-builders between the Marine Corps and the community an essential and invaluable mission. In the 1970's, internal as well as external outreach was also important. The Marine Corps Reserve had to deal with an Active Duty force that did not always see the value or professionalism of reservists, many of whom had volunteered to return to active duty and go fight in the jungles of Vietnam. Although educating the active duty force about the value, capability and readiness of reservists was not a new task for MCROA, the situation in the 70s was exacerbated by shrinking budgets, the end of the draft and fallout from political decisions made in the execution of the war.

In 1970, then Secretary of Defense, Melvin Laird, introduced a new DoD policy that assigned greater roles and responsibilities to the Reserve components.[2] The idea behind Total Force, which went into effect in 1973, was that the Reserve components were no longer forces in reserve, but would go to war alongside active duty forces in the event of a national emergency. In theory that meant that the Reserves should have access to modern equipment and be provided with "mirror-image" training that the active duty received. It was a noble goal, and one fully supported by MCROA. However, in practice, implementing the Total Force concept was much easier said than done. Making Total Force a reality has consumed more than three decades of effort. Total Force meant that the Armed Forces had to reassess everything, from the way Reserves were funded and managed to internal cultural perception about Reserve capabilities. It would not be an easy road. In the struggle to bring Total Force from paper to practice, MCROA, in a rare moment, would go before Congress and publicly air its disagreement with the Marine Corps over the implementation of the new policy.

In the early 70's another new policy created still further challenges for MCROA and the Reserves in the areas of recruiting and retention.

By the summer of 1971, the draft, the nation's primary method of bringing young men into the Armed Services, was due to expire. Many saw the writing on the wall; in the aftermath of Vietnam finding the fiscal and public support for a large military force during peacetime (a recurring theme in the aftermath of all America's wars) was going to be difficult. Government committees began looking at alternatives to the draft even before America's involvement in Vietnam was officially over. In 1973, the policy known as the All-Volunteer Force (AVF) went into effect. As a result the military now had to rely on volunteers instead of draftees to fill its ranks. MCROA and many others were concerned about the implications of the AVF on the Corps and the military as a whole, especially in the areas of recruiting and retention.

Before 1973, long queues of draft-eligible men waited to join the Reserve and Guard units because they recognized both the Reserve and the National Guard as a way to satisfy their military obligation and concurrently pursue their civilian careers. They also realized that the Reserve forces would not be activated en masse to fight in Vietnam. When the draft ended, the lines of applicants disappeared and Reserve recruiting difficulties and shortages began.[3] Instead of relying on non-prior service for the bulk of its accessions, Reserve components increasingly came to rely on prior-service men and women to help them meet end-strength goals. Meanwhile, the active duty component was also faced with recruiting challenges of its own. After the draft, the Marine Corps still aimed to attract a "few good men" to its ranks. That meant attracting an enlisted population of high school graduates and the best and brightest college men to fill out the officer corps. The Marine Corps turned to MCROA, as well as other USMC supporters, to help both on the reserve and the active duty recruiting fronts. From the start of the decade the connection between MCROA members and the civilian communities and the Corps' reliance on that connection was clearly evident.

At the 1970 national convention, Commandant Gen. Leonard F. Chapman Jr., asked the members of MCROA, as Marines and as part of the civilian community, to carry the story of the dedication of the Corps to other Americans—especially young people, in order to give them a positive example and guidance. Through outreach, it was hoped that MCROA members would not only help the Marine Corps find suitable recruits, but also help bridge the growing gap between the Pentagon and the American people in the aftermath of Vietnam.

The call for MCROA's recruiting help was reiterated in the minutes from MCROA's 1975 national conference.

"There are more than 587 Marine Corps affiliated organizations helping with the recruiting effort. These are MCROA, Marine Corps League, Marine Corps Correspondents, etc."

During the conference, BGen. E.B. Meyer, who presented the Marine Corps Manpower and Recruitment report to the membership, asked MCROA to help recruiting in the following ways:
- Referrals
- Participating in high school career days
- Helping recruiters in contacting local officials
- Helping OSO's onto college campuses

Reserve recruiting was an especially challenging task, because in the 70s reservists did not enjoy many of the same privileges as their active duty counterparts. Medical coverage, exchange access, educational funds and insurance were just some examples of "bennie" gaps that existed between reservists and regulars. In addition, trying to attract prior-service Marines to the Reserves was hard because of fallout from Vietnam. As any student of history knows, organized Reserve units were not called out for service during Vietnam, although many individuals volunteered to go to the fight. Furthermore, because joining the Reserves in the 60s was a way for some to escape the draft, many active duty Marines regarded reservists as barely one step up from draft dodgers, or "weekend warriors" who were not squared away. Indeed, many MCROA members said they held that view when they came off active duty, but as soon as they joined a unit or became active in the organization the perception of the "weekend warrior" quickly faded.

MCROA members, as leaders in their communities, with business, political and educational contacts, were pressed into service. Both MCROA and Marine Corps national leadership called upon the greater membership to assist recruiters in their districts spread the word to the youth of their communities about the benefits, honor and glory of pinning on the eagle, globe and anchor.

MCROA's efforts at outreach were not aimed solely at potential future Marines, but also Marines on active duty and veterans. Since the Reserve was relying on prior-service Marines to fill out its manpower requirements, MCROA members crafted presentations geared toward active duty Marines who were close to getting out. In many ways the argument for joining the Reserves in the 70s were much the same as they were in the aftermath of the World War II—join the Reserves and maintain the unique Marine Corps connections, camaraderie and esprit de corps. MCROA also tried to help returning veterans and their families readjust to "normal" life after Vietnam. MCROA efforts included helping veterans find work, dealing with paperwork and offering basic moral support. One especially successful program MCROA launched was visiting veterans hospitals. The program was one of four "community relations" programs approved by MCROA in 1971. In addition to visiting Marines "who have made considerable sacrifices for us and their Country and who are now in Naval or VA hospitals," MCROA members started:
- A Marine Youth Foundation aimed at encouraging citizenship, discipline and physical fitness in the country's youth
- A Marine and Family Assistance program
- A program to support the ROTC program

Indeed the ROTC program was a controversial topic in the early 70s. Many universities and colleges, such as Harvard, Yale and Dartmouth, withdrew support, course credit and academic status for the program that provided roughly half of all officers on active duty at the time. ROTC program chairman Col. R.M. Hewlett sent a personal letter requesting MCROA's help to association president, MGen. Sidney McMath.

MCROA chapters were asked to not only educate themselves about the issue, but go out in the community to build-up support. The plea that went out to the membership in March 1970 sounded dire.

"If we do not make the max effort NOW, the adversaries of our citizen-soldier concept will succeed in the abrogation of the ROTC program," read the front-page article in *The Word*.

By mid-decade, the impact of the AVF and Total Force policies was still being hotly debated. Overall, Selected Reserve end-strength across all services continued to drop and reached an all-time low of 788,000 in 1978 compared to over 950,000 in 1964.[4] In some instances reserve recruiting quotas were lowered simply because the Reserve could not supply enough bodies to meet the demand. In 1974, at the 48th annual MCROA convention, the membership passed a resolution calling on Congress to reinstate the draft as quickly as possible.

"Whereas this climate favorable to maintaining the required strength of the Armed Forces on an All-Volunteer basis does not exist today. Now therefore be it resolved, by the members of the Marine Corps Reserve Officers Association in conference assembled, that the President of this Association communicate to Congress a request for a study of the feasibility of a Reserve Draft."

The frustrations over AVF spilled over into the application of the Total Force policy as well. The scramble for resources with which to procure equipment and training for active duty and Reserve Marines became very tight. Reservists and MCROA leadership soon began to feel that although Total Force existed on paper, its spirit was not being honored in practice. When MCROA's national president Col. Jack M. Frisbee and Chairman of the Board, MGen. Arthur B. "Tim" Hanson testified before the Total Force Study Committee on 5 March 1974, Hanson had some tough words about how Total Force was going.

"Now in light of the fact that the Secretary of Defense has stated that the total force concept is a total force policy, it appears clear to us that every one of the Services, including the Marine Corps, must bend every effort to make this policy become a reality. We are publicly telling the people of the United States that we are giving them 30 percent of their active forces for five percent of the defense budget.

But we can't do it if the regular establishment, from the Secretary of Defense down to the staff sections of the various regular services, is not supportive of this policy. We can't do it if we are short changed in recruiting funds and recruiting efforts," Hanson told the committee.

Ultimately improvements in training, equipment and funding would be realized, but it would be slow going. Indeed the struggle for parity between the Reserves and the active duty forces would continue well into the 1990s.

Finally, it's important to mention one MCROA community outreach effort that has gained sustained national attention over the last three decades and that is the Marine Corps Marathon. In 1976, Maj. Jim Fowler, a MCROAn, helped start what was then known as the Marine Corps Reserve Marathon. The race was geared at combining physical fitness and publicity for the Marine Corps in one event. Twenty-four years later the Marine Corps Marathon has become the sixth largest marathon in the nation and is considered one of the best "first-timer" courses to run. Indeed, everyone from presidents to generals to housewives has participated in this event over its long history.

THE 1980'S—MODERNIZATION AND PARITY

Two themes dominated MCROA's agenda in the 1980's—modernization and professional development. As the Marine Corps continued to struggle with and adapt to the realities of an All-Volunteer Force and the Total Force policy, the number one issue for the whole Marine Corps would be upgrading equipment. New names such as Cobras, Hornets, and LCACs would be added to the devil dog vernacular. On the legislative front MCROAns battled for resources for the Reserve Force, which was still trying to catch up to regular units and squadrons when it came to pistols, tanks and aircraft.

As one former president of MCROA described the decade, "it was a competition for dollars. The active duty Marines wanted to have the training money and the latest equipment, not to accommodate the Reserves."

Artillery weapons were of Korean War vintage, some reserve pilots were flying aircraft that were no longer in the active duty inventory and spare parts were hard to come by. Although the Reserves were used to getting "hand-me-downs" from the active duty Marine Corps, with the implementation of the Total Force policy, interoperability became a hot button issue for the Reserve.

Traditionally, MCROA has prided itself on trying to work issues out with Marine Corps leadership internally, but this wasn't always possible. In 1982, MCROA leadership felt they had to go "outside the family" in order to address equipment concerns. The Reserve's only transport squadron only had half of its authorized 14 aircraft by 1982. In a letter to Congress, MCROA president Charles Swope wrote, "In order for the Total Force Concept to be effective, the Reserve forces require sufficient modern equipment to meet mobilization day commitment to augment the regular forces as a ready partner in time of national emergency. As the role of the Marine Corps Reserve evolves to provide total force capability, the stated requirements of KC-130 aircraft are needed to provide sufficient air refueling and transport ability to adequately support the contingencies placed upon them." Congress listened. By 1985, 12 brand new KC-130T Hercules were authorized to go directly to the Reserve. That was enough

planes to not only fill out the original squadron at Naval Air Station Glenview, but also stand up another squadron in Stewart Airport Reserve Training Center, in Newburg, NY.

"The Marine Corps has experienced a deficiency in tactical air refuelers, particularly in the Reserve. Hence, Congress ordered a program to procure the Reserve aircraft squadron designated as Marine Aerial Refueler Transport Squadron (VMGR)-452," read the July/August 1985 article in *The Word*.

Another significant legislative milestone in MCROA's history occurred in 1985. At the time the Graham-Rudman-Hollings Law threatened retirees' cost-of-living allowances. In effect the law killed the 3.1 percent COLA for 1985 and would have reduced lifetime retired pay through 1991 by 22.5 percent. Since this issue reached beyond the interest of MCROA alone, the association, along with 11 other military organizations, banded together to form The Military Coalition, or TMC. TMC, which is still around more than a decade later, focused on personnel issues rather than platforms or force management. By the 1990s, TMC represented 24 different military associations with a membership base of more than 3 million. MCROA "realized that sometimes it takes the combined strength of many organizations to effectively represent their members' interests before national decision-makers" wrote MCROA's executive director, Larry Gaboury in the Mar/April 1995 issue of *The Word*.

When MCROA was first founded, political activism was its foundation. Many of MCROA's members were members of the Senate or the House. Politically savvy men like Melvin Maas and Tim Hanson were as comfortable in the halls of power as they were in their own living rooms. However, as MCROA matured, legislative involvement, although still important, became secondary. Instead, during the 1980s, MCROA's at-

Brigadier General Leland W. Smith with actor and AF Brigadier General Jimmy Stewart at the Veterans Day Celebration in Birmingham, Alabama, November 11, 1981.

tention would turn inward. Professional development, membership and chapter growth became the focus.

In the 60s MCROAns held their first regional seminar in San Diego. More localized meetings such as this, to discuss military issues of the day or MCROA business became more common in the 70s. But it was not until the 80s when the concept of professional development became institutionalized within MCROA and the Marine Corps as a whole.

Nowhere was the emphasis on professional development more noticeable than in the association's own publication, *The Word*. Over six decades *The Word* had gone from a four-page flyer to newsletter to glossy magazine. By the 1980s ads, articles on history, strategy and Reserve training exercises filled out the usual fare of chapter news, ALMAR announcements and death notices. In some ways *The Word* was MCROA's version of the *Marine Corps Gazette*. Unfortunately, the new look of *The Word* was not meant to last.

Throughout the history of MCROA, sustaining the viability of the association's marquee publication was always a challenge. But in the 80s the lack of advertising revenue and a publisher who promised more than he could deliver lead to the suspension of the magazine's publication. In 1984, MCROA president John Coyne sadly informed the membership that *The Word* would return to a "newsletter" format, known from then on as *The Word (-)*. The struggle to make the magazine both viable and relevant would continue over the course of the decade. In the late 80s MCROA tried to entice members' input–especially contributions from junior officers–by offering a prize for articles selected for publication. The program didn't exactly work as well as MCROA leadership had hoped. In the Mar/April 1988 issue of *The Word*, President Allan Millett's frustrations were given voice.

"If members of the association do not write for their own professional journal, they surrender the field to those who are more interested in illusions than ideas. If you think the Marine Corps Reserve is nothing but a photo opportunity, then *The Word* as it now is should make you happy. If you think you want to be represented by a better magazine, then do something about it," Millett stated in his monthly column.

It would not be until the 1990s that MCROA would see a return to the "glossy" format of its beloved magazine.

But the magazine was not MCROA's only trouble spot during the 80s. Internally, there was much grumbling by the membership that MCROA had lost its direction, credibility and reason for being. Building a membership base had been a perennial issue for the association, but after reaching an all time high of 5,500 members between the 1970s and the 1980s, MCROA would be hard pressed to crack the 5,500 member ceiling. The battle for a stable membership seemed to be aggravated by internal impressions that MCROA had become an "old colonels club" and was nothing more than a rung on the promotion ladder for its leaders.

"It's hard to pin down, but of all the organizations I belong to I get the least pleasure and known result while paying the highest dues for a MCROA membership," wrote one unhappy member in 1982.

The debate over MCROA's relevance came to a head in January 1984. In perhaps one of the longest president's messages on record, Col. Mitch Waters tried to address the concerns that had been plaguing MCROA for some years. In a two-page address to the members, Waters argued that MCROA was what members made of it.

"This message, however, is meant to reply to each of you that MCROA's national officers are aware that there are negative comments regarding the association and that we are addressing each one, attacking them head on! It is easy to sit in the stands, grandstand quarterback, and to complain and second-guess. Let me offer an alternative. If you do not like what is taking place, do something about it! Get involved. Join us and help MCROA meet the challenge; recognize that each of these concerns becomes an opportunity to improve and strengthen your association.

Your involvement can make a difference! Make a personal commitment to MCROA! It's your professional association," Waters told all MCROAns.

THE 1990S—THE GULF WAR AND BEYOND

John Kaheny barely had time to assume his new position as president when he got the word. There was going to be a war and he, along with the 3rd Civil Affairs Group he commanded, was needed in Southwest Asia.

When Saddam Hussein invaded Kuwait in the summer of 1990, there was much speculation among reservists (as well as US civil and military leadership) about whether or not reservists would be called. If President George Bush went ahead with the call–up, which would be the largest in US history, it would be the first time since the Korean War that Reserve Forces would be employed in a combat zone en masse. Although Kaheny, along with 39 officers and enlisted Marines from the 3rd CAG, were some of the first reservists to go into theater, eventually as many as 13,000 Marine Corps reservists would find their way to the barren battlefields of the Kuwaiti desert and thousands more would be called upon to backfill and support the active troops serving at the tip of the spear.

But unlike World War II, MCROA did not suspend its activities, even though many of its officers and members were called to the service of their nation. Kaheny's second in command, Col. Kevin Doyle, filled in as president. Other members submitted articles to *The Word*, outlining everything from legal considerations Marines had to be aware of to histories of the region US forces were headed to.

One of Doyle's first acts was to rally the membership around the Marines and their families that were involved in the Gulf War.

"There is much to be done to support our troops deployed, to support their families at home, to present a strong and unified presence in our communities, to foster the professional development objectives of our MCROA Foundation and to advance the value of our association," Doyle wrote in his president's message of January 1991.

Another way MCROAns helped fellow reservists throughout the war was simply by offering advice and the "Reserve perspective" to their active duty counterparts. Many MCROAns, on station in the Gulf, through individual effort, helped smooth the way and iron out problems for themselves and fellow reservists throughout Desert Storm and Desert Shield. Kaheny recalled how he started hearing about reserve pay backlogs while he was in the Gulf. He said he not only tried to address the issue with Gen. Walt Boomer, whom he was working for at the time, but Kaheny was also able to get word back to MCROA back home and mobilize the association to address the issue as well.

US troops, both active and reserve, served with great honor and distinction in the Gulf. They prosecuted a war that took hours instead of weeks and sustained the lowest casualty rate ever. However, upon their return home, the US military had to gear up for another fight. This battle was not a new one, and characteristically took place after every major US military engagement. The issue that dominated MCROA's agenda in the post-Gulf years was manpower and endstrength. And once again MCROA would go to the mat for a robust Reserve.

After the war ended it seemed everyone was involved in examining the correct force mix for the active and reserve forces. The foremost proponent of cutting back reserve and active duty numbers seemed to be the Department of Defense, not Congress, as had been the case in the past. In June 1991, Col. Doyle, who by then had been elected to his own term as president of MCROA, was called before the Senate Armed Services Committee to testify on the proposed reduction of 9,000 Marine Corps Reserve billets.

"The Selected Marine Corps Reserve is less than one fourth the size of the active Marine Corps. Since the passage of the National Security Act of 1947 the Marine Corps has served the nation well with a structure of 3 active divisions and wings and one reserve division and wing. The ratio in other services is irrelevant to the issue of whether the Marine Corps Total Force is appropriately sized for the perceived threat. MCROA believes that the current structure remains appropriate and we know that the congress believes this as well.

"Just as a concept of equitable sharing of reductions is illogical in the context of inter-service needs, so too is it illogical intra-service. Should the congress choose to reduce the size of the active Marine Corps structure on some rational basis then, in the case of the Marine Corps Reserve, it would appear logical that the effect would be an increase in the size of the Marine Corps Reserve to retain the same total force capability rather than a decrease," Doyle told the committee.

"Of more immediate concern than the proposed elimination of nearly one quarter of the SMCR structure over a six year period, however, is the proposed reduction of some 3,000 selected reserve billets in the coming year.

"MCROA does not believe that the Marine Corps would propose such reductions if it was not under some DoD mandate to reduce the active structure. Would a Marine Corps that mobilized and deployed two entire reserve tank battalions to Southwest Asia—battalions which served with such distinction—propose deactivating all but two companies of those battalions if it was not under some external pressure?"

Doyle concluded his testimony by saying, "MCROA believes that Congress uniquely appreciates the proven performance of the Total Force Marine Corps and will provide the necessary funding to man, equip and train the SMCR near term and long term."

Congress did end up cutting overall Reserve endstrength somewhat, but not nearly in the numbers called for by the Pentagon. And by the time MCROAns elected their first and to date, only female president, Col. Susan Malone, SMCR numbers held at just over 42,000 Marines.

However, that security was to be short lived. As budgeting got underway for the fiscal 1994 year, endstrength once again seemed to be in danger of shrinking. And once again MCROA mounted a strong defense, appearing before Congress in the summer of 1993. This time association president Col. Frank A Tauches Jr. delivered the MCROA message.

"This year's Department of Defense FY94 budget proposed a Marine Corps Reserve endstrength of 36,900. This is 5,400 fewer billets than the current endstrength, a 13 percent decrease in one year. Such a precipitous drop is almost certainly inexcusable without wholesale RIFs. Most importantly, the size and scope of the planned reductions take out more capability than is prudent," Tauches said. "Such deep cuts will hinder the Total Force Marine Corps' ability to comply with the current national military strategy and unified command forward operating tasks."

And if anyone doubted that MCROA had any credibility before Congress, the results of the debate, delivered in Jan. 1994, proved otherwise.

"WE WON! WE WON," read the exuberant first line of MCROA's legislative update. "MCROA fought for it on the hill, it was one of our resolutions, HQMC endorsed the same, the Bottom Up Review agreed, the Senate Armed Services Committee recommended it and finally the Congressional Conference Committee decided on a Marine Corps end strength of 177,000 active and 42,200 Reserve."

Indeed, Reserve endstrength would remain at the 42,000 mark for the rest of the 1990s, until the Quadrennial Defense Review in 1997 reduced reserve endstrength by 3,000.

One other important piece of legislation was finally passed in 1994. The Reserve Officer Personnel Management Act was signed into law in October 1994 and became fully effective in 1996. ROPMA, as the bill was known, was companion legislation to the Defense Officer Personnel Management Act that went into effect for active duty officers in 1980. ROPMA would be the first major overhaul of reserve officer personnel policy since 1954 and was designed to provide compatible personnel management system for reservists and active duty officers. MCROA had long been a supporter of the bill and during the course of many conventions passed resolutions urging its passage. Although there were many factors that influenced the eventual ratification of the legislation, the association's long-standing support for its cause—the betterment of the training, equipping, managing and employing of the Reserve—was illustrated once again in this instance.

Equipment battles also continued in the aftermath of the Gulf. In the summer and the fall of 1994 the issue was tanks. Reserve tank battalions were critically short of M1A1 tanks after the Gulf War. During Desert Storm, Reserve tankers made a name for themselves by compressing seven weeks of training on the M1A1's into two and a half weeks, then arriving in the Gulf and obliterating a whole Iraqi tank battalion while sustaining no casualties. But by 1994 the reserve tankers only had eight out of a required 32. During the FY95 budget process MCROA sent out a "call to arms" message, mobilizing its members to write and call members of Congress and deliver the message that if the Reserves are to continue to perform they need the equipment with which to train. And once again Congress heeded the call. The FY95 Defense Appropriation Act provided for 48 new tanks for the Reserve force.

In the 1990s, MCROA has continued to emphasize professional development for its membership and took steps to provide increased support of that program. In 1990, the MCROA Foundation was created to further the aims of professional development. The foundation has depended on donations for survival and has sponsored seminars, essay contests and other programs to stimulate the thinkers of the Reserve Corps to speak and write about issues of personnel, training and strategy.

MCROA still continues to participate in The Military Coalition and its members are still called upon to serve as advisors to Marine Corps leadership on issues that pertain to the Reserve and their integration into the larger Marine Corps.

Unfortunately, MCROA is still waging a battle for an active and growing membership. Because there are not the same legislative fireworks in the 90s that there were in the 50s, because many Reservists are so busy being out there, breathing life into the Total Force Policy, sometimes it seems that MCROA is a shadow of its former self.

In the latter half of the decade many an officer has asked, "What has MCROA done for me?"

One former president of MCROA has a ready answer.

"Part of what reservists enjoy today is the fruit of what others have done," said MGen. Mike Coyne. "MCROA has been the best and really the only voice Reserve officers have. It has been our collective voice"

ENDNOTES

1. Marine Forces Reserve Public Affairs, "A Brief History of the Marine Corps Reserve," http://www.marforres.usmc.mil.

2. The bulk of this section is quoted almost directly from the pamphlet, "A Brief History of the Marine Corps Reserve Officers Association," published by MCROA in 19XX.

3. McCahill, The Marine Corps Reserve, A History, p. 48.

4. Norman Polmar & Thomas B. Allen, World War II; American at War 1941–1945,   p. xii.

5. 4th Marine Division Battle Staff Historical Detachment, History of the 4th Marine Division 1943–1996, Marine Corps Historical Branch, p. 6.

6. A MCROA History; 50 Years of Service to Country and Corps, p. 10.

7. MCROA's Newsletter, April 1946, p.1.

8. A Brief History of the Marine Corps Reserve Officers Association, p. 15.

9. 4th Marine Division Battle Staff Historical Detachment, History of the 4th Marine Division 1943–1996, Marine Corps Historical Branch, p. 29.

10. McCahill, p. 188.

11. A Brief History of The Marine Corps Reserve Officers Association, p. 25.

12. Millet, Allan, Semper Fidelis; A History of the Marine Corps.

13. At this point in history all Marine Corps officers received an initial reserve commission. Those who wanted to become active duty had to augment.

AUTHOR'S ACKNOWLEDGEMENTS

I hope this book will serve as a source of pride for past, current and future members of MCROA. I sought to write this material based on the major themes that characterized each of the seven decades that MCROA has been in existence. If I have left something out, the fault is mine, but I think the final work paints a picture of an association that has remained dedicated to its founding principles of fighting for a Reserve Force that is well trained, equipped and integrated.

Whenever you take on a project like this, you don't take it on alone. And because this book is built upon the memories of many men, I would like to single out a few for special thanks in their help in making it possible.

First and foremost I would like to thank Tom Green and George Hoffman for thinking of me and giving me the distinct honor and privilege to participate in this project. I would also like to thank Tom for giving me access to the association's archives and trusting me with what often were the only copies of MCROA's historical papers.

Thanks must also be given to all the members who sat for interviews and gave me background and context for my research.

I am especially grateful to Charles Swope and John Kaheny for sharing their collections of *The Word* from the 1980s and 1990s. Those issues were critical in the completion of this work and I thank you for holding on to all those magazines.

Thanks also to Mitch Waters, John Coyne and David Leighton—your memories, connections and insights were invaluable.

I would also like to acknowledge that this opportunity would not have been possible had I not had the privilege to cover the Marine Corps Reserve beat at *Navy Times*. Of all the services I have covered, I have had the best time with the Devil Dogs. I am proud that over the years many of the Marines I met as a reporter have now turned into friends. Your dedication humbles me, your friendship honors me, and your service to this country makes me thankful.

Finally, I would like to dedicate this work to Col. William P. McCahill. He is the true historian of the Marine Corps Reserve and was the first interview for this project. His warmth and openness were a joy to experience and his love of the Corps is unequalled.

PAST NATIONAL PRESIDENTS
*Deceased

*1926 MGen Melvin J. Maas,
USMCR Ret**

*1951 Col Joseph Chambers,
USMCR Ret**

*1952 LtGen Karl S. Day,
USMCR Ret**

*1955 BGen Carlton Fisher,
USMCR Ret**

*1958 BGen John L. Winston,
USMCR Ret**

*1960 MGen Douglas R. Peacher,
USMCR Ret**

*1962 MGen Robert B. Bell,
USMCR Ret**

*1964 MGen Arthur B. Hanson,
USMCR Ret**

*1966 BGen Russell A. Bowen,
USMCR Ret.*

*1968 BGen Leland W. Smith,
USMCR Ret.*

*1969 MGen Sidney S. McMath,
USMCR Ret.*

*1970 Col Marvin Schacher,
USMCR Ret.*

*1971 Col Stuart F. Nelson,
USMCR Ret.*

*1972 Col Howard N. Feist, Jr.,
USMCR Ret.*

*1973 MGen Jack M. Frisbie,
USMCR Ret.*

*1974 BGen Robert S. Raisch,
USMCR Ret.*

*1975 MGen Hugh W. Hardy,
USMCR Ret.*

*1976 Col John A. Gose,
USMCR Ret.*

*1977 Col John J. Ward,
USMCR Ret.*

*1978 Col John H. Bemis,
USMCR Ret.*

PHOTO NOT AVAILABLE

1979 Col Russell Harwood,
USMCR Ret.

1980 Col Wes Santee,
USMCR Ret.

1981 Col Vincent J. McGarry,
USMCR Ret*

1982 Col Charles E. Swope, Jr.,
USMCR Ret.

1983 MGen Mitchell J. Waters,
USMCR Ret.

1984 MGen John T. Coyne,
USMCR Ret.

1985 Col David J. Leighton,
USMCR Ret.

1986 Col Herbert N. Harmon,
USMCR

1987 Col Allan R. Millett,
USMCR Ret.

1988 Col Conrad F. Mauge,
USMCR Ret*

*1989 Col Harry Sullivan,
USMCR Ret**

*1990 Col John M. Kaheny,
USMCR Ret.*

*1991 Col Kevin M. Doyle,
USMCR Ret.*

*1992 Col Susan Malone,
USMCR Ret.*

*1993 Col Frank A. Tauches, Jr.,
USMCR Ret.*

*1994 Col Bradley T. MacDonald,
USMCR*

PHOTO
NOT
AVAILABLE

*1995–96 Col James T. Ragsdale,
USMCR*

*1997 Col J. Anderson Harp,
USMCR*

*1998 Col Robert L. Hudon Jr.,
USMCR*

*1999 Col Allan F. Cruz,
USMCR*

SPECIAL STORIES

Project: Build bridge 4th Combat Engineer Bn. "A" Co., Camp Lejeune, NC, July 1968. (Courtesy of J.L. Davis)

BON VOYAGE, MARINE!

by Col J. Dale Hollabaugh, USMCR (Ret)

I was sitting at my desk at HQMC in May 1966, very pleased with myself after receiving order to 3rd MarDiv (RVN)–Infantry, finally ending my "payback" tour for having achieved my MSEE at USNPGS in '63, when the phone rang. With the past three years in the Supply Department of HQMC, buying ground comm equipment for the Marine Corps, added to the prior three years in Monterey, I had been out of the FMF and the Infantry for six years—two thirds of my "career" to date—an eternity, but I was going to set it right with these tickets to the fight!

"Hello, Comm–Elect Div of the Supply Dept, HQMC, Captain Hollabaugh speaking!"

"Sir, this is the office of the Vice Chief of Naval Operations for Anti–Submarine Warfare Vice Admiral Martell, and he would like to speak with *you!*"

Now my wife Nada and I knew the Martell family as their daughter, Ritchie, used to date one of my companymates. Nada and the Admiral's daughter became fast friends as they regularly made the trek from greater DC to Annapolis in the daughter's *intermittent* Morris Minor our First Class year—before the parkway was completed—a lot of pushing! The Martell's were a gracious lot and were instrumental to our June Week wedding and reception (but just let me say, the O–9 and this O–3 maintained the proper distance!)

"Captain Hollabaugh—Dale?"

"Yes sir!"

"Understand that you have orders to Vietnam. When do you detach?"

"June, sir."

"Well, Mrs. Martell and I would like you and Nada to come over to our quarters and have lunch at your earliest opportunity so that we can wish you a proper farewell."

"Aye-aye, sir. Did the Admiral have a date in mind?"

"How does this Saturday sound?"

"Sir, that's perfect." (No matter the date and what we were doing, it would be perfect!)

"Great. Do you know how to get to our quarters?"

"No sir, but I'll find out, sir."

"Well, we're in the group of quarters off Constitution Avenue—Quarters X."

"Aye-sir, we'll find it."

"Good, Dale, and don't forget to bring the children."

"*Uhh*, aye-aye, sir, we'll see you then."

I immediately called Nada and her response was, "…the *children*???" We agreed, we had a lot to do before "this Saturday. The children were Bret (eight) and Linda (five).

For the next few days, meals and family time were filled with proper dress, table etiquette, speech, answers to typical questions, etc.—a type of Naval Academy/flag charm-grooming cram course Marine-style. For example, one of my consistent inputs was, "No matter what Mrs. Martell serves, everyone eats it! I don't care if it's worms on a bun, everyone will smile and woof it down and thank her for it graciously!" There was no doubt what I was going to wear (SSC), but we discussed the appropriate attire for Nada and the children at an Admiral's lunch in quarters in May, ad nauseam.

The day finally arrived and, of course, there was an inspection before we left the house. A few changes were made and we were off—lecturing all the way from Springfield, Virginia. I had asked many people about the quarters near Constitution Avenue and thought I knew exactly where I was going, but when I got into the area, it wasn't obvious, and there was no way that this *male*, Marine Captain was going to go up to any Navy O–9's door and ask *directions*. After a few frantic minutes, I found a suitable spot to park (i.e. for an O–3 in O–9 country, by a dumpster) and moving the family briskly, we approached

1st LT J. Dale Hollabaugh, 1960.

what appeared to me to be the entrance to the proper quarters. It was the proper quarters all right, but unfortunately we quickly discovered it was the kitchen entrance when one of the Admiral's cooks gathered us in and called a Side Boy to escort us down a long spotless white marble–floored hallway to the parlor, while the other cooks and Side Boys smiled and snickered throughout the working spaces in the quarters!

The parlor was beautiful but very formal, with a resplendent Jacobean bench–type couch, sitting chairs and mahogany display cabinets with wonderful objet d'art—and an absolutely magnificent Persian rug covering most of the hardwood floor. Moments passed as the children looked in awe around this beautiful room and as I did a terrific ASW search pattern on the beautiful multi-colored rug. We heard a voice and so I gave a "standby" to the troops and turned to face the door, when I noticed that my right foot was stuck to the deck (that is rug), kind of a suction feeling. I quickly placed my left foot and forcible picked up my right foot while making a reflexive sweep of my right sole with my right hand, picking up something gooey. I glanced at my hand in horror, as the smell hit my nose—yes, it was *dog dirt*! Just then, the Admiral sailed around the corner, resplendent in his whites and gold bars, and said, "Hi Dale, nice to see you." I met the Admiral's outstretched right hand with the only good hand I had, my left, while hopping forward on my clean left foot and said, "Nice to see you sir—uh, where's the head?" He looked incredulous and I glanced over at the troops and all three of their mouths were gaping, lower jaws on the floor, undoubtedly thinking, "Dad's finally lost it!" When I hit the marble hallway, I couldn't keep hopping because I thought I'd slip, so favoring my right foot, I limped to the head leaving a little brown spot on that beautiful white marble deck every other step for what seemed like 50 yards! (This part is better acted out—picture it!)

After cleaning my spit-shined shoe and hand thoroughly, I ventured out into the hall with handfuls of paper but someone had cleaned up my tracks, and following voices, I found my way to the dining room. The Admiral met me and, shaking my hand vigorously, explained that he was very sorry, that "the dogs (two miniature poodles) were clipped that morning and are always nervous and prone to accidents after their haircuts." (I had missed their calling card due to the ornate pattern of the rug.) Mrs. Martell was there also and expressed her apologies as she seated us around this huge, gorgeous mahogany table. The children were distracted by the fact that there were at least fifty candles burning at all levels in the dining room, making for a lovely atmosphere, as Nada and I tried to courteously pay attention to the seating so that hopefully we could get our kids to seats where we had a commanding position. Nada and Linda ended up on one side and Bret and I on the other, with the Martells on each end.

And so, after pleasantries, the stewards began to appear, scurrying right and left. As I remember, salads were served to the side and the main dish brought out quickly––it was a large tomato stuffed with a tuna mixture, which looked wonderful ad Nada and I were pleased, but neither one of our glaring looks could cause the children to look happy. They didn't say anything, of course, but Mrs. Martell picked up on their disappointment and spoke up immediately, saying, "Linda, you probably would rather have something else, wouldn't you? How about a hot dog?" (Linda's favorite main course.)

Nada or I said, "Oh no, she has had this before and will be happy to eat it," as Mrs. Martell hit the buzzer on the floor. Out popped a steward's head and Mrs. Martell said, "a hot dog please." No sooner had he closed the door than Mrs. Martell saw Bret's eager, anticipating face and said, "Oh, Bret, what's your favorite sandwich?" "Hamburger." Buzz goes the buzzer, out pops the steward, "A hamburger too, please."

"What do you normally eat when you go to a restaurant? A grilled cheese sandwich? Would you like that?" Little heads nodded "yes", grown-up heads shook, "no". Buzz! "Two grilled cheese sandwiches, please." Nada said, "Mrs. Martell, the hot dog and hamburger will be fine, pleeease." Needless to say, the messmen didn't mind our leaving since in about five minutes we had turned the place into a McDonald's at noon-time!

The rest of the afternoon is kind of a blur, like the haze of a hangover or combat, except that I do remember one other significant event. We were shown the *front* door by the Admiral and how we calmly (Daddy, our car isn't back here!) returned to our car in the rear of their quarters without getting challenged or shot is another story for another time!

Bon Voyage, Marine! Bring on Vietnam!

A FLIGHT TRAINING TALE

by Ira V. (Red) Babcock

During the month of September 1943, I was undergoing operational flight training in SBD–5 type aircraft Cecil Field, NAS Jacksonville, Florida. We were also training rear seat gunners. All of the student pilots had just graduated from flight school, myself included.

During the latter part of our training, we did some night flying, which included night glide bombing and tactics, etc. Our standard flight pattern at Cecil Field was 1000 ft. above sea level on the downwind leg.

This story concerns one of the student pilots and his gunner.

One night, our two students were returning to Cecil after completing their flight for the evening. On the downwind leg, the engine quit. The student pilot suddenly remembered that he had forgotten to switch fuel tanks. So, he promptly switched tanks to one that had fuel in it. The engine caught just before the student pilot, student gunner and airplane hit the ground. Fortunately, both pilot and gunner were able to walk away from the crash with only minor cuts and bruises, and deflated egos. They were examined that night at the sick bay and returned to flight duty.

The same pair went flying again the next night. When it was time to return to Cecil Field, at the end of the flight, the pilot entered on the downwind leg and made a normal landing. When he taxied up to the flight line and shut the engine down, the line crewman asked him where his rear

VMA 321 Anacostia Naval Air Station, Washington, DC. Commanding Officer Carrol Morris.

seat man was. The pilot looked around and said, "I don' know," and the search was on for the missing gunner.

The gunner came walking into the main gate of the air station around 1:00 AM with his parachute slung over his shoulder. It seems that when the pilot reduced the throttle at the 180° position on the approach, the gunner thought that the engine had quit again, so he bailed out. He wasn't about to ride that monster down to another crash landing.

THE VIET CONG NATIONAL GUARD

by Robert D. Tuke

During March 1971, Combined Action Company 2-4 was experiencing numerous incursions in its area of operations, across the Hoi An River from an island controlled by the Viet Cong known as Cam Tahn Island. On night we decided to interdict one of their principal routes of ingress and egress. We set up a platoon–size, expanded L-shaped ambush along a tree line and a graveyard. Shortly after setting in, but before it could dig in, the platoon spotted movement nearby. Soon the night quite was pierced by the unmistakable sound of mortar tubes firing.

The CAP Marines and PF's hunkered down awaiting the explosions of impacting rounds. The explosions did not come. Instead, audible splashes in the paddy water and "thunks" in the mud were all that could be heard. The Marines and PF's directed a hail of gunfire toward the assumed firing positions of the mortars, knowing their luck might not be so good next time. Still, the next volley of rounds could be heard leaving the tubes.

Once again, everyone crawled inside their helmets. But again, nothing happened but thunks and splashes. This went on for at least seven volleys from three tubes. As it became obvious that something was dreadfully wrong with the VC mortar attack, the Marines and PF's began to maneuver and drive off the enemy, with no friendly casualties. By then, the only worry had been that someone might be hit by a falling projectile.

The next morning I carefully policed up more than 20 unexploded 60mm mortar rounds. Each was intact, each was serviceable, and each still had the safety pin securely in place in the warhead. After blowing the rounds in place, we all enjoyed a laugh, having concluded that we had just survived a surprise mortar attack by the "VC National Guard."

DOUBLETIME TRAINING

by J. Todd Miles

In the mid–1980s the Marine Reserve faced a very bad shortage of generator and refrigeration mechanics. WES–47, Det A (later MWSS-473) at NAS South Weymouth was tasked with support of operations with mechanics that they just didn't have.

LtCol J.T. Ferland, UMCR, told his staff to come up with a solution. Funding was approved by 4th MAW to fly two staff members from the Marine Corps Engineer School to NAS South Weymouth for two consective drills. The experts from MCES were able to teach the repair of the most common breakdowns in just 32 hours of instruction, so that operators could do double duty as mechanics. They didn't learn to fix everything, but on just one operation they fixed four generators, two refrigerators and an ice machine that would have otherwise been deadlined for the duration.

LIBERATING KUWAIT CITY

by Timothy M. Hanson

During the Gulf War I was the Intelligence Officer (S-2) for 5th Battalion, 10th Marines and also served as the Assistant Operations Officer (S-3Z) for the battalion. Our unit entered Kuwait the first night of the ground war and provided artillery fire for the units of the Second Marine Division in their advance through the minefields and north into Kuwait.

As the First and Second Marine Divisions routed the Iraqi forces we raced north to stay in range and provide artillery support. We even did a "hip shoot" from the convoy where we basically pointed our guns in the direction of the enemy and adjusted fire as necessary. We even had a Kuwaiti Liaison Officer with us. He had been a college student prior to the war and managed to escape Kuwait several weeks after the occupation.

The Marines advanced to the southern edge of Kuwait City and were told to hold there and allow our Arab allies to liberate the city—under no circumstances were

An instructor from Marine Corps Engineer School teaches a Marine from WES-47 how to recharge a reefer unit with freon.

we to enter. Being a good Marine and a "salty" first lieutenant, I dutifully acknowledged those orders and then disobeyed them by taking our Kuwaiti liaison officer into Kuwait City to look for his family and to see if they were still alive.

One of the greatest memories of my life is entering Kuwait City from the west. Where 12 hours earlier had been a despotic military government with posters of Saddam Hussein everywhere and tyrannical rule, it was now a free city. Kuwaiti flags had been banned by the Iraqi military, but as we entered the city the flags were everywhere. They were hanging from the windows of buildings, were mounted on poles and waved from vehicles by AK-47 toting Kuwaiti freedom fighters, they were on benches and plastered everywhere, even on people.

As we drove through the city in our Humvee, people of all ages would run up to our vehicle to express their gratitude with a touch, a handshake, a smile or shout a phrase or two: "George Bush Number One!" "USA good!" or something in Arabic with a smile and a wave. Prior to the war, these people were probably anti–American as most Arabs and Muslims were, but were now proudly pro–American.

We drove to our liaison officer's home in a lovely section of Kuwait City, and there he met several neighbors who had not been fortunate enough to escape. His family, which consisted of eleven children, was not

Marines on break during the Gulf War, Al Jabal, Saudi Arabia, December 1990.

there. Some sisters had been sexually assaulted by Iraqi soldiers and their whereabouts were unknown, other had escaped when the ground war started, others had simply disappeared. His mother and father's fate could not be determined. We reluctantly returned to our units as nightfall approached.

The next day we took him back again and this time he stayed. I don't know what happened to him or his family. My last sight of him was of him walking with his arms around his neighbors, back into the courtyard of his house.

I mentioned to the Kuwaitis how much I liked their flags and, according to custom, they insisted I take one. It is my most prized war trophy, because it was given so willingly and meant as much to them to be able to give it to me as it did for me to receive it. We left the city later and I have never returned. I hope to return someday, find my Kuwaiti Liaison friend and share my experiences with my wife.

Liberating a city is one of the most humbling, yet enriching experiences anyone could have. My experiences as a Marine and in Kuwait have had an effect on me and I thank God for his delivering my fellow warriors and me from the war safely.

Visit of ACMC to Camp Pendleton for Operation Beat Tempo in 19-20 August, 1969; MGen Donn J. Robertson, Commanding General, 4th Marine Div HqNuc; General Lewis Walt, Assistant Commandant of the Marine Corps; Colonel J.J. Campbell, OIC, Annual Training Duty Detachment.

A Fraternal Brotherhood

by James J. Campbell

Occasion: 1st Marine Division Association Dinner Meeting Installation of General Raymond G. Davis (Medal of Honor Winner) as President of the Association.

Where: Old Garden City Hotel, Long Island, New York

When: March 1966

During a break in the festivities, I was approached by an elderly couple in the hall just outside the ballroom. Identifying themselves as Mr. and Mrs. Bauerschmidt, they asked me whether the presence of so many Marines in Dress Blues and Evening Dress could have any connection with the 1st Marine Division. I then assured them it did in fact and explained the reason for the celebration.

At this point, Mr. Bauerschmidt took out his wallet and showed me a photo of their son, William, a Marine Lieutenant. He told me their son had been killed in action on Pelelieu and that they had never met anyone who had served with him. He asked if I thought there might be someone in attendance who might have done so. I asked them how they happened to be at the hotel and they responded that they were staying there just that one night while on a trip from their home in Pennsylvania.

I asked them for the number of their room and promised I would summon them if I could find that someone. With the help of Bill Layden, an Association Member of the committee for this function, I located Master Sergeant Pat McInerney, USMC (Ret). He told me that Lt. William Bauerschmidt, his Platoon Commander, had died in his arms on Pelelieu. Pat was his Platoon Sergeant. He said he would love to meet his parents. I escorted them from their room to the Ballroom, introduced them to Pat McInerney who seated them at his table. While they chatted, I informed Ed Herlihy of this wondrous happentance. He, in turn, informed Generals Davis and Murray, who invited the Bauerschmidts to join them on the dais. As they were introduced and seated, they received a rousing standing ovation from the throng in attendance. I doubt there was a dry eye in the ballroom!

This incident was reported in a local Long Island newspaper and a local radio station a few days afterward, thanks to Ed Herlihy, whose son was a Marine at the time. Special note: Marine Lieutenant William B. Bauerschmidt, 022663, USMC, was awarded the Silver Star for heroic action on Pelelieu.

BIOGRAPHIES

Marine Corps Reserve Policy Board, USMC HQ, April 1968. (Courtesy of Col. J.J. Campbell)

OLEN S. AKERS, Colonel, born Jan. 3, 1937 in Pontotoc, MS. He served from June 1956-December 1957 (NAVCAD Class 25-56), Whiting, Barin, Corry (Last SNJ Class), Beeville (TV-2; F9F-8); Active Duty, F9F-8 and A4D-2; VMA-311, January 1958-October 1959; VMA-121, October 1959-April 1961; Reserve, VMA-124, FJ-4 Memphis, May 1961-February 1963; VMF-351, Atlanta, F8U, June 1967-July 1975; Anglico, Miami, July 1975-August 1976; Aviation Staff Group, Memphis Co. MABS-42, Memphis 1977-79; Aviation VTU, HQ MC 1982-88.

While in VMA-121 at Eltoro and Iwakuni, won CNO Safety and CMC award. Also Completed AVN Maint. Off. School in 1959. He received all the usual decorations.

His education includes a BBA in accounting from the University of Mississippi in 1963, CPA. MCAA, MCROA, lifetime member.

Retired as VP marketing, Unisys, where he was employed for 32 years. He and wife Jan have no children.

ANTHONY A. "AL" ALICO, Major, born Jan. 1, 1916 in Buffalo, NY. Trained at Parris Island, 1942; Quantico, VA, 1943, 25th Res. Officers Class. He served with Schools Co. Montford Point, Camp Lejeune, NC; 8th Svc. Regt. HQ Co. CO in Nagasaki, Japan.

Landing in Japan with the 2nd MarDiv., 5th Amphibians Corps, 8th Svc. Reg. shortly after the dropping of the bomb, he along with a contingent of black Marines were assigned to Nagasaki to cleanup for the landing of the 2nd MarDiv.

After several months they were sent to San Diego in preparation for separation from the Corps and eventually home.

After active service he became the proprietor of the Paragon Shoppe in Orchard Park (a men's and boy's clothing store) and the Arcade Men's Shop, Arcade, NY. He retired in 1977 into a full time real estate broker in New York State. At present he is a volunteer reader to the sight impaired on the Niagara Frontier Radio Reading station.

He is a life member of MCROA and has received Citizen of the Year, 1990 in Orchard Park, NY and the Melvin Jones Fellow Award presented for the dedicated humanitarian services presented by the Orchard Park Lions Club.

His education includes BA Sociology from Canisius College, Class of 1939.

He married Mary Sullivan and is the father of three boys and one girl, Ken, Tom, Barb and Bill.

ELMER ALBERT "DADDY WAR BUCKS" ANDERSON, Colonel, born Feb. 27, 1922 in Chicago, IL. Attended Armour Institute of Technology, enlisted in the USMC March 1942 and served as aviation mechanic, ordnance personal on the USS *Long Island*, CVE for VMF-223 during Guadalcanal, Coral Sea Campaign. Commissioned in the V-5 program, he served with VMF-121 and VMFN-543 before reporting to Korea in 1951.

He flew 15 missions from K-1 before designated embarkation's officer moving supplies via LSDs, to K-18. Established oceanography for POL lines at K-18 for base operations. Flew 35 missions from K-18 and X-83 directing air and naval gun fire for the MLR zone.

Awarded the Distinguished Flying Cross, three Air Medals, Rifle Sharpshooter and Expert Pistol Medals and other campaign and commendation medals. Col. Anderson retired in 1982.

He returned to CONUS 1953 and was employed as marketing manager for Illinois Bell and continued his association with the Marine Corps, flying AD-1s, F8Fs, F9Fs at NAS Glenview. He commanded the 2nd Angilico Grp. of Chicago and attended staff courses Quantico, Coronado.

He has been married for 53 years to Rosanne and they have one son, one daughter and one granddaughter.

OTTO AUGUST ANDREAE, Lieutenant Colonel, born Jan. 16, 1913 in New York, NY. Upon graduation from San Diego boot camp, 1943, was part of the 1st Marine platoon to study the hush-hush radar equipment, which later he taught to Navy and Marine officers in the Marine Air Corps. Also stationed at Utah State University at Rogan, UT, April-June 1942, Ward Island, TX, June-December 1942, US Naval Tech Training Center; January-June 1943, Officers Training at Quantico, VA; and US Naval Tech Training Center, MOTG 81.

He is the founder and chairman of the Board of Therma-Tron-X, Inc. and has been married to Jean (Nee Zion) Andreae for the last 56 years and they have four children, 17 grandchildren and five great-grandchildren.

GEORGE ANTHONY ARETAKIS, Lieutenant Colonel, born Nov. 1, 1917 in New York, NY. Commissioned July 21, 1942 as a member of MCROA and took staff courses at Marine Corps Schools and graduated from Quartermasters School 1942. He also served at Parris Island, Camp Pendelton, CA, 5th Roc., Quantico, III Amphib. Corps, Saipan and Tinian, 3rd OCS.

CO, VTU, CO, ENGRG CO, disbursing and purchasing officer Hawaii 1942. He was recalled for Korea Incident Landing in Inchon. Awards include Rifle and Pistol Expert. He is a long time member of MCROA, III Marine Air Wing Purchasing & Disbursing Officer and Air Group Supply Officer. After discharge he became an accountant.

The Aretakis family had six who served in WWII. Brothers: Aristomenis, Agamemnon, Emanuel were Marines. Eustachio Cosmo (brother-in-law) was the Navy PO. His mother was heralded by the *New York News* and *Post* for having six members who served. Brother George, a retired LtCol, was recalled for Korea. He was in the III Marine Air Wing as a Navy Air Supply Officer. A lifetime McRoan, he brought the brothers together at Camp Lejeune, Camp Pendleton and Quantico, where he graduated from Quarter Masters School.

George was a VTU Commander and Korean Veteran.

GEORGE WILLIAMS AYERS,
Colonel, born Dec. 21, 1939 in Portsmouth, VA. Trained OCS, TBS, Quantico, VA and served with MAG-16 Okinawa/Vietnam 1962-63; 4th MarDiv. (Infantry, Artillery, AAV, Armor) 1964-76; Reserve Naval Construction Force (Seabees) 1978-83. Command and Staff College 1983-90; HQMC 1988-91; I MEF 1991.

He was CO, Ammunition Co. 4th FSSG, Co. D Co. 8th Tank Bn., advisor, Commander, Reserve Naval Construction Force, HQ I MEF (Gulf War).

He has receive several military awards including the Legion of Merit, Meritorious Service Medal, Navy Commendation Medal and SMCR Medal w/ Silver Star.

He is currently a professor, neuropsychiatry and behavioral science at USC School of Medicine. He also has a doctoral degree from Tulane University, attended staff courses Naval War Colleges, Armed Forces Staff College, Army War College and Adjunct Faculty USMC Command Staff College. He and wife, Melissa, have one son and one daughter.

IRA V. "RED" BABCOCK, Colonel,
born Jan. 28, 1920 in Great Valley, NY. He enlisted in the regular Marine Corps, Nov. 6, 1940 at Detroit, MI; boot camp at Parris Island, SC; duty in St. Thomas, VI in VMS-3; went to Flight School in October 1942, graduated at PNS Aug. 1, 1943; attained a commission November 1943.

Went to South Pacific January 1944 and flew SBDs in VMSB-244, flew 41 missions in the Bismarck Archipelago Campaign. Instructed primary flight training at NAS, Memphis, TN in 1945, then RelActDu January 1946. Joined VMF-441 in Niagara Falls, NY until recalled to active duty in October 1951.

Following recall, he was an instructor pilot with VMIT-21 in Miami, FL; took helicopter training at Ellyson Field, PNS September 1953; duty in Japan and Korea in VMO-2 and VMO-6; duty in operations at MCAS, Miami, FL, as air sea rescue officer; had one year as the Officers Club OIC. RelActDu June 30, 1958.

Following release was a founder and principal investor in a civilian helicopter operation, Call SUN LINE Helicopters in Miami. In 1961 moved to Dothan, AL where he went to work for the US Army at Fort Rucker as a aircraft accident investigator. He retired from the Army civil service in January 1980.

Reserve duties included: CO, HMM-765, (twice), CO, 28th Staff Group (Aviation). Flew the H-34 that carried the Lockheed camera crew that took pictures (still and movie) of the first launch of a Polaris Missile from a ship off Cape Kennedy. Accumulated 8,500 accident-free flight hours in various fixed and rotary wing aircraft.

His decorations include the Good Conduct Medal, Distinguished Flight Cross, five Air Medals, Bismarck Archipelago Campaign w/star, American Theater w/star.

Education includes courses at New York University, University of Georgia, University of Arizona and the Aviation Offers Safety Course at University of Southern California. He completed Reserve Command and Staff Course at Quantico, Reserve Landing Force Planning and the Amphibious Warfare School at Little Creek, VA. He also completed the Marine Corps Command and Staff College Extension Course.

He is married with two children, fully retired and living in Dothan, AL.

VICTOR E. BIANCHINI, Colonel,
born Feb. 21, 1938 in Pedro, CA. Commissioned in the PLC (Law) program in 1960, he served with the 1st Marine Aircraft Wing in Vietnam, as a trial and de-

fense counsel, the wing informational services officer, the wing civil affairs officer and as wing photographic officer doing additional duty as a combat correspondent. He flew 61 missions with various squadrons.

For his Vietnam service he was awarded the Bronze Star Medal w/Combat "V," three Air Medals, Combat Action Ribbon and numerous additional campaign and unit awards. He also served as the CO of the 4th Force Recon Co., the CO of Mobilization Training Unit (MTU) CA-12 (Law), as a courts-martial judge and the OIC of Individual Mobilization Augmentee (IMA) Detachment, Sierra Judicial Circuit, Camp Pendleton, as a special staff officer, MTU Project, Kansas City and as the deputy inspector general and OIC of IMA Detachment, US European Command, Stuttgart, Germany.

He was awarded the Joint Services Commendation Medal for service with USEUCOM and the Legion of Merit for service as a special investigator with the Office of Inspector General, HQMC, during Desert Shield/Desert Storm. He is a qualified jump master, entitled to wear the Navy/Marine Corps Parachute Badge and the Combat Aircrew insignia. He was also awarded the Vietnamese Parachute Badge. He retired in 1991 after more than 31 years of service.

He has served as the national judge advocate general and councilor at large on the National Board of MCROA. He is a life member of MCROA and was first a member in 1961.

His education includes a BA degree from San Diego State University and a juris doctor degree from the University of San Diego School of Law and is a candidate for a masters degree in forensic sciences.

He has been actively engaged in education for over 30 years, serving as an adjunct professor at both the university and law school levels and was the founding dean of an accredited California law school. He is a retired US Magistrate Judge and a former US Commissioner. He currently serves as a Superior Court Judge in San Diego, CA. He has combined service as a judge of over 27 years.

WILLIAM L. BIRDWELL, Colonel, born July 24, 1931. Platoon Leaders Class, 1951, San Diego; 1952 Quantico; Basic School, 2DBC 1954; Amphibious Courses, San Diego; CMD and Staff, Quantico; Naval War College I and II; 1st Bn., 12th Marines; 1st Bn., 14th Marines; 12th Staff Group, CO MTV-53, 1983-84.

Memorable experiences include Desert Operations; amphibious landings; President Gillespie Chapter (Los Angeles) MCROA. He received the National Defense and Organized Reserve Awards.

He has BBA, grad work, business administration, education administration and is a certified financial planner. He is married with three sons and three granddaughters.

ROBERT A. BLACK JR., Captain, born Feb. 20, 1942 in Charleston, SC. Appointed Mid'n, USN, 1959; commissioned in USMC 1963. Served as XO, MarDet, USS *Randolph* (CVS-15); rifle platoon leader, exec. off., CO, Co. K, 3rd Bn., 2nd Marines; S-4 BLT 3/2; liaison off., Commando Marine, Toulon, LanForMed 3-65; LSU Cdr., Carib 3-66; RU Cdr., 1967; HQ. Cmdt, CO, Co. E, 2nd Bn., 1st Marines (Rein), RVN; S-2, CO, Co. B, 1st Bn., 1st Marines (Rein), RVN; staff off., HQMC.

Honorably discharged 1969. Awarded Silver Star Medal (Khe Sanh), Cross of Gallantry w/Gold Star (Battle of Hue), Combat Action Ribbon (Quang Tri), two PUCs (Da Nang TAOR, Hue City), Commendation (Haiti and DomRep). Designated an Olmsted Scholar.

While a midshipman, was member of standby boarding teams for naval blockade of Cuba during 1962 missile crisis, underwent airborne training and served in Royal Belgian Navy. Later, as infantry officer, served as 2nd Marines liaison briefly in 1965 DomRep operations. As Logistic Supply Unit commander provided humanitarian relief in Haiti and DomRep. After completing

Def. Lang. Inst., was assigned to 1st MarDiv. in Vietnam and participated in operations throughout Northern I Corps, 1967-68 (Phong Luc, Phu Kich Islands, Quang Tri City, La Vang Tri, Base Area 101, Nui Con Thien, Phu Bai, Hue City, Upper Perfume River, Street w/o Joy, Operation Pegasus/LZ Stud, Khe Sanh Hills 558, 950, 881S, 689).

On entering CivLant, undertook doctoral studies in international relations at Columbia University as Lehman Fellow and International Fellow, followed by positions with the Institute on Western Europe, Council on Foreign Relations, The Conference Board, Columbia University Graduate School of Business, Council on Learning and the Young Presidents Organization. Created Ranger Corporation, a closely held firm assisting businesses in preparing for and doing business offshore. Later set up RB/C, an international consulting group focusing on business design, systems to support same, and transaction management. During this period, operated in and from various countries.

Received BS in engineering from US Naval Academy, did graduate work at George Washington University, American University and received various graduate certificates and degrees from Columbia University. Taught as adjunct at Lehigh University and Ramapo College; frequent adjunct lecturer at various colleges and universities around the world.

Author of various papers, articles, book chapters, books, etc. Has been member of MEA, VFW, MOFW, Huguenot Society, USNAAA, Society of International Fellows, ISA, inter alia. Served on various association boards and helped establish The Business Design Group. Currently president of RB/C, a member of TBDG and associated with Corporate Transitions International.

An accomplished fencer (1963 MD 3-Wpn champion/Iron Man, 1964 Olympic Trails foil semi-finalist), continues to compete and win medals as member of Salle Santelli and referees extensively.

REED ROBERT BONADONNA, Lieutenant Colonel, born April 22, 1955 in Brooklyn, NY. Trained PISC and OCS, 1979. Served 2/8, 8th Marines, RTR DISC, 25th Marines, 1/25,

MECEP Prep School, Naval War College.

Memorable experience was expeditionary war duty in Beirut, 1981. His awards include the NAM, USMC Expeditionary, Humanitarian Service, Navy Unit Commendation, SSDR.

He has PhD in English. He is married to Susan and has three sons: Erik, Devon and Luke.

DONALD E. "BOOMER" BOOMERSHINE, Colonel, born Oct. 5, 1931 in Brookville, OH. Commissioned in the OCC program, served MASS-1 2nd Mar. Air Wing and MACS-8 3rd Mar. Air Wing, Miami; senior air director and flight briefing officer GCI/GCA. Battery CO, S-2 4th Ba. 14th War. Senior Umpire for air during a number of Marine/Navy amphibious exercises.

The board of directors of MCROA. Since 1984 a designated information officer for the US Naval Academy; Alabama Committee for the Employers Support of the National Guard and Reserves; National Veterans Day vice president since 1988.

His education includes a BBA from Bowling Green State University, graduate in banking degree from Rutgers University and did graduate work at Northwestern University and the University of Oklahoma.

Federal Reserve Board of Atlanta-Birmingham Branch, served two terms from 1991-97, board chairman 1993 and 1995; National Board Bank Marketing Assn. 1968-71. Earned Airborne Wings at Fort Benning at 45.

Currently president, Better Business Bureau, covering 41 of 67 counties in Alabama. He and his wife, Patti, have two sons, Jeffrey and Andrew.

GERARD J. BOYLE, Colonel, born June 26, 1949 in Cambridge, MA. Commissioned 1972. He served with 2nd FSSG, 2nd MarDiv., 3rd FSSG, 2nd MarDiv., 3rd FSSG and MCDEC on active duty from 1972-85. Chief Trial Counsel with 3rd  FSSG and MCDEC. With the Marine Corps Reserve from 1985 to present serving in Reserve Affairs Division, HQMC; Officer in Charge of Marine Corps Mobilization Station, Top Sham, ME during Operation Desert Storm. Presently Marine Corps Liaison Officer for Naval Readiness Command One, Newport, RI and Officer in Charge of Team Yankee, A joint service medical training unit at Westover Air Reserve Base. Awarded Meritorious Service Medal, Navy Commendation Medal.

From 1996 to present serving as the Marine Corps Coordinator for the Employer Support for the Guard and Reserve Committee in New Hampshire and as the Marine Corps Aide de Camp to the Governor of New Hampshire. Active in MCROA, Marine Corps League and the American Legion.

His education includes a juris doctor and master of public administration degrees from Suffolk University and a bachelor of science degree from Boston College. He is a graduate of the USMC Command and Staff College, the US Naval War College and the NATO School. He is presently a criminal trial lawyer and member of the New Hampshire Judicial Council. Col. Boyle resides in Plymouth, NH with his wife and three children.

JOHN F. BOYLE, Major, born Oct. 20, 1954 in Boston, MA. Commissioned in the PLC program in 1976, his active duty included H&MS-14, 3rd LAAM Bn. MACG-28; 1st Tracked Vehicle Bn., 3rd MarDiv.; and MAG-49, Det. A, 4th MAW NAS, South Weymouth, MA. He also served five years with MCMS, Topsham, ME. He is a graduate of the Naval Justice School and the Marine Corps Command and Staff College (non-resident course). He was awarded a Navy Achievement Medal and A Navy Commendation Medal.

His education includes a BA from Boston College in political science; a MA from Pepperdine University in human resources management; and a JD from Franklin Pierce Law Center in Concord, NH.

He is married to Kate Havern and they have three children: Jonathan, Colleen and Michael. He works at the Boyle Law Office in Plymouth, NH.

WILLIAM RICHARD "BILL" BREMER, Colonel, born Jan. 5, 1930 in San Francisco, CA. He received his BS (business administration) from Menlo College in February 1952 and headed for Quantico, VA, as a Marine private assigned to the 4th OCC. When commissioned, he completed the 14th SBC and Air Control School and was ordered to Korea as a GCI air controller, MGCIS-1, 1st MAW, Kunsun.

He was assigned as an exchange controller to the 608th AC&W Sqdn., USAF, Chodo Island and recorded eight enemy aircraft intercepts. Released from active duty in 1954, he remained in the Reserve holding a variety of billets and commands through February 1982, whereupon he retired from the Corps. He holds the MSM.

He received his JD, University of San Francisco, School of Law in 1958 and was admitted to the California Bar. He has since been in the private practice of law, serves as a hearing officer for the county of Marin and as an arbitrator and a Judge Pro Tem for the courts of San Francisco and Marin counties.

He was a board member and president of the Marines' Memorial Club, San Franscisco; a life member of the Navy League and San Francisco Council president, Northern California State president, a national director and is currently a national deputy judge advocate. He is a life member of the NOUS and served as San Francisco commandery commander, national judge advocate general and commander general (national president) 1993-95, the first Marine officer to hold that office.

He was elected a councilman and mayor of the town of Tiburon; served as an officer and director of the Marshall Hale Memorial Hospital Board, San Francisco Children's Hospital Board, the Bridgeway Plan for Health, as a member of the board of Bay Area USO and on the board of the Center of the Pacific Rim, University of San Francisco. He is a life member of MCROA, ANA, ROA, TROA, Naval Reserve Association and the Naval War College Foundation wherein he serves as a regional vice president, northern California. He a past Commodore of the Corinthian Yacht Club.

He is married to the former Margaret (Peggy) Herrington. They have three children: Mark (deceased), Karen and William Jr.

GARNETT P. BROY, Colonel, born Aug. 16, 1952 in Baltimore, MD. Commissioned 1976, he trained at The Basic School, via PLC, January-June 1976, Fort Sill Arty. School, July-November 1976; Command & Staff College, Reserve Course, 1991-92; Landing Force Staff Planning, MEB, LFTC, PAC 1994; Expeditionary Warfare Trng. Grp., Landing Force, CSS 1996.

He served with the 3rd MarDiv., 105 Btry. D/S Bn., as FO, 1977; 3rd MarDiv., Base Ranges, Camp Schawb Range Officer, 1977; MCB, 29 Palms, CA, Human Affairs Officer, 1978-79; K Co. 3/25, Plt. CDR and XO, 1979-November 1984, special projects officer, MCDEC, 1990, asst. mobilization plans officer, Training & Education Center, Quantico, VA, 1990-91; 4th Civil Affairs Group, Det. Commander, 1991-93, Commander, OIC, Philadelphia Mobilization Center, 1994-95; Reserve Support Program, 4th Dist. Logistic Officer, 1996-present.

Personal decorations received include Organized USMCR Medal, Sea Service Deployment Ribbon, NDSM, Navy Commendation Medal, Defense Meritorious Service Medal, LOM, Volunteer Service Medal.

He is a 25 year member of MCROA, member of the National Military Intelligence Assn., Marine Corps Intelligence Assn. and current member of the Army & Navy Club, Washington, DC.

He is currently employed with the Maryland State Police, sergeant, supervisor with the Human Resources Division. He is active in the community in the Red Cross, Maryland Food Committee and currently serving on the board of directors of the Lutherville - Timonium Recreational Council.

His new reserve assignment will be assistant chief of staff recruiting support, Eastern Recruiting Region and Recruiting Support Officer, 4th Marine Corps District.

He and his wife, Jacqueline Brown Broy, have a daughter, Jessica (16) and son, Garnett (14).

GARY F. BURCHFIELD, Lieutenant Colonel, born April 16, 1936 in Scottsbluff, NE. Commissioned 2nd Lt, USMCR, from University of Nebraska NROTC program in June 1957.

Active duty included TBS at Quantico, Communication Officers Orientation Course, Quantico, followed by duty with 2nd MarDiv. as CommO for 2nd Pioneer Bn., 1958-59. After release from active duty, he joined 2nd Comm. Support Bn., USMCR, in Chicago. Other reserve assignments included CO of 26th Rifle Co., Minneapolis, MN; CommO for 23rd Marines, Alameda, CA; XO and CO of 4th MWSG, Lincoln, NE. Additionally, from 1964-74, was a member of the USMCR Smallbore Rifle Team and participated in rifle matches throughout the US including three trips to the national matches at Camp Perry, OH.

He retired from USMCR with 27 years of service in 1984. Military awards include AFRM, Organized Marine Corps Reserve Medal and Marine Corps League Commandant's Medal.

He presently works as a freelance writer and public relations consultant. He and his wife, Phyllis, have four children and five grandchildren.

WILLIAM V. "Bill" BURGESS, Lieutenant Colonel, born March 26, 1943 in San Francisco, CA. His training includes Quantico, VA, 1965-70, PLC, TBS; 1975-76, Command and STUA (Res); 1983 Naval War College NP Rd. He served with 1st MarDiv. 2/1 "F" Co., 1967-68, Vietnam, C Co., 4th Recon Bn. (Res); company CO and platoon commander, Reno, NV; 23rd Marines S-2,

Alameda, CA; 6th MAB CA G-2.

He was a combat platoon leader, Marines; Recon Commander, Company of Marines; M-60 machinegun co. cmdr. He also receive awards including Purple Heart, CAR, Vietnam CG.

He is a senior financial advisor with American Express and is a Navy/Marine Corps multi-generation family.

CHRIS W. BURKHART, Lieutenant Colonel, born Detroit, MI. Training includes OCS, Quantico, VA, December 1979; TBS, Quantico, June 1980; Basic Comm. School, Quantico, March 1981; Reserve AWS, June 1990; MC Command & Staff non-resident, June 1996.

He served with MMU-1, 3rd FSSG Comm. Co., 3D LSBN, 8th Comm. Bn., 2nd LSBN, 3rd MarDiv. Comm. Co, MCTSSA, 4th Tank Bn., MWCS-48 Det. B, I MEF CE.

He is a 1991 Phase II Honor Graduate of Reserve Counterintelligence Course. In 1992 completed Joint Psychological Operations Staff Planner Course. He has received the MSM, NAM, SMCR Medal and NDSM.

He is currently a computer scientist, Software Acquisition. He also is a life member of MCROA, has a BA in biology and MA in management information systems. He is married to Atsuka and has three children: Rosemarie, Joanna and Nana.

EUGENE DUNCAN "DUNK" CAMERON, Lieutenant Colonel, born June 16, 1923 in Syracuse, NY. Training included Chapel Hill, NC, September-December 1942, Hutchinson, KS, December 1942-June 1943, Corpus Christi, TX, June 1943-September 1943, Ft. Lauderdale, September 1943-December 1943; Santa Barbara, CA December 1943-February 1945. He served with VMF-221, HMR-261, VF-212.

In the spring of 1945 he completed 150 combat missions in the Pacific and Korea and shot down three Japanese aircraft. Awards include the Distinguished Flying Cross w/2 stars, Air Medal w/6 stars and Presidential Unit Citation w/star.

He is retired and has three children, two step-children and three grandchildren.

JAMES J. CAMPBELL, Colonel, born Aug. 16, 1923 in Brooklyn, NY. He enlisted April 7, 1942 and was commissioned in August 1943. He attended Officer Infantry School (Comm), Fort Benning, GA and Naval Communications School, Harvard U.

He served overseas with MAG 33 in Pelelieu and Okinawa campaigns. He joined the 2nd Communications Co., USMCR, NY, in February 1952 and served as CO (1957-60). Served as a member of 1st Staff Group (ground), USMCR, NY 1960-63, then CO, 6th Communications Bn., Fort Schuyler, NY, 1963-66. He then joined VTU 1-7 (Intel), NY. He was member of Captain's Promotion Board, July-August 1967, instructor, Extension School, Quantico, VA, July-August 1968. He was assigned as OIC, Reserve Liaison Unit, ATD Det., 4th MarDiv., Camp Pendleton in 1969-70. Member of VTU Staff 12-8 when appointed CO of 16th Staff Group (Ground), San Diego, CA, 1971-73.

He served as member of 1st Marine Corps District Policy Boards in 1959, 1960, 65, 66, 69 and member of Marine Corps Reserve Policy Board, HQ MC in 1968-69. He retired on June 30, 1974.

He is a member of TROA, Marine Corps Association and life member of MCROA. His civilian experience includes service with the NYPD, 1946-62, Lynbrook Public Schools, NY, 1962-691; Chapman College, CA, 1969-72; Administrator, California Public Schools (Oceanside, Goleta, Palm Springs), 1972-81.

He holds BA, St. Francis College, NY and MA Adelphi University, Garden City, NY. He lives in La Jolla, CA with Jane, his wife of 50 years. They have six children and 11 grandchildren.

HERBERT E. "GENE" CAPRON, Lieutenant Colonel, born Aug. 3, 1921 in Geneva, NY. He trained at NAS, Pensacola and served with VMSB-931, 932; VMJ-1; VMJ-2.

Some of his memorable experiences and achievements include: Air Medal, SBD, SB2C, F4U, F6F, the "Banshee" in Korea, Naval Aviator, Instrument Green Card, FAC 1st Marines.

He and his wife, Janet have two sons, Richard (Methodist minister) and Jay (manager of campus coffe shop, a VA Tech).

RAY A. CARLSON, CWO4, born Oct. 12 1945 in Pensacola, FL. Training includes Parris Island, 1970, Camp Lejeune, 1970. He served with C&E Bn., 29 Palms; HMM-766; HML-776; MWSG-47.

He was mobilized for Desert Storm, sent to NAS Cubie Point, Philippines and received a Certificate of Commendation.

At present he is a medical physicist and president/owner of Radiological Physics Service, Inc.

He and his wife, Pola San, have one son, Raymond.

PETER GERARD "HANNIBAL" CARVER, CWO3, born Feb. 4 1961 in Boston, MA. Training includes Parris Island, November 1981; Cherry Point, November 1982; RWOBC, January 1994; Quantico, July 1994; Little Creek, VA, PME, January 1997. He has served with WE5-2F, H&HS Sqdn. Picas Beaufort, WES-47, MWSS-473, MWSS-474.

Memorable experiences and achievements include PI graduation, January 1982, PLT 2098; WO appointment, October 1993 as 1390 fuels officer; first assigned as Utilities Plt. OIC, MWSS, Desert Shield Mobilization.

Awards received include: NAM, SMCRM, AFRM, MUC, NDSM and Sea Service Deploy Ribbon.

He is currently a Massachusetts State Parole Officer. He and his wife, Elizabeth, have two children, Sean and Maeve.

JEROME GARY COOPER, Major General, born Oct. 2, 1936, Lafayette, LA. From 1958-70 he was an active duty Marine Corps officer. He earned the Distinguished Service Medal, LOM, BSM, two Purple Hearts and the RVN Gallantry Cross w/Palm, Silver and Bronze Stars.

In Vietnam, he became the first African-American officer to lead an infantry company into combat in USMC history and later commanded a Marine Reserve unit. He was promoted to major general in 1988 and returned to active duty as director of Personnel Procurement, HQ, USMC.

As a private citzen (from 1970) he has served as director and corporate officer of his family's 70-year old insurance company and funeral home. In 1976 he and other local citizens founded Alabama's first and only minority-owned and operated national bank. He served on the Alabama State Legislature; was appointed commissioner of Alabama State Department of Human Resources; appointed by President Bush in 1989 as the assistant secretary of the Air Force for Manpower, Reserve Affair, Installations and the Environment. He participated in the planning of Operation Desert Storm.

He served as vice-president and senior vice president of David Volker and Associates, an engineering and architectural firm. 1991-94; in 1994 President Clinton selected him to serve the US as ambassador to Jamaica; currently, he is the chairman of the board and chief executive officer of Commonwealth National Bank and serves on the board of GenCorp, a Fortune 200 corporation.

Cooper has served on the board of Talladega College and Spring Hill College, been recognized by the NAACP, B'Nai Brith, the city of Mobile AL, the Secretary of the Navy, the University of Notre Dame and Omega Psi Phi Fraternity. He is a graduate of the University of Notre Dame and has BS in finance. He also completed a special program for senior managers in government at Harvard University. In 1990 Troy University awarded him an Honorary Doctorate of Law.

He is married to Beverly Martin (Coleman) of Richmond, VA, a transportation and health care consultant. He is the father of three children: Patrick (graduate of Yale Law School), Joli (graduate of Wharton School of Business) and Gladys (former Marine Corps officer and a graduate of the J.L. Kellogg School of Business).

DANIEL B. CORTS, Lieutenant Colonel, born Sept. 17, 1933 in Stoughton, WI. Enlisting in the Marine Corps in Billings, MT in July 1952, he completed boot camp MCRD San Diego and infantry training at Camp Pendleton, CA, joining the 3rd MarDiv. FMF; A-1-3 deployed to Kaneohe Bay, HI in June 1953, then Yokohama, Japan one month later. Supporting the UN Command, Korea, A-1-3 occupied the Mount Fuji area and conducted amphibious exercises on Okinawa, Iwo Jima and elsewhere. Returning to CONUS September 1954, he reported to Camp Pendleton as Troop Handler, 2nd ITR. After leading Marines through infantry and cold weather training and coaching rifle shooters, he completed his enlistment July 1955.

Active Reserve by 1957, Corts affiliated with 10th Inf. Bn., Seattle, WA. In Montana, he trained in two rifle companies, 36th (Butte), 58th (Billings), and 1st Tank Co. (Missoula). He served as platoon sergeant and platoon leader upon commissioning as a lieutenant, November 1961. As a captain, he commanded Communication Support Co. FMF, Indianapolis, IN, 1967-69. Employed in Washington DC as a research psychologist, US Office of Personnel Management, he affiliated with MTU DC 02, serving as CO, 1980-84. Projects were accomplished for HQ USMC and MCCDC, Quantico, VA.

Training schools completed: M48A1 Tank, Comm. Officer, Amph. Warfare, Command and Staff College, LFTU - Coronado and Little Creek, National Defense University, Jacksonville, FL and two tours at the Naval War College, Newport, RI. He was a controller for firing exercises on Vieques, PR.

His awards include the GCM, Organized Marine Corps Reserve Medal and other medals for overseas and UN service during the Korean War. He is a life member of MCROA and ROA and a MCA member.

His education includes a BA and MA in experimental psychology, from the University of Montana. Other professional studies were completed, including experimental design at the Massachusetts Institute of Technology, Cambridge.

WILLIAM A. COTI, Colonel, born July 7, 1931 in New York, NY. Enlisting USMC 1948. Korea: September 1950-October 1951 (barman/light machine gunner). Discharged November 1952.

USMCR 1953-63: squad leader/platoon commander E/F Co., 2/25, USMC 1963-68: Company Commander (CONUS) F Co. 2/5; (Vietnam) K Co. 3/9, E Co. 2/9, H&S Co. 2/9. Recommended for Navy Commendation Medal w/Combat V.

USMCR 1968-91: CI Officer. 1971-77: Provided CI, Intelligence and Security briefings to USMC detachments and commands throughout Europe, Africa and Near East; provided operation security for CINCUSNAVEUR commands and N-5 sites; performed ACDURTA as Acting Naval Attache, US Embassy, Bonn, Germany (1973-76). 1977-83: CI Branch, MCDEC, Quantico: Defined requirements for a new family of CI equipment for USMC CI Teams - subsequently purchased; exploited Soviet material outCONUS and collected foreign intelligence (hostile naval/ground activity) for USN/USMC.

Awarded Certificate of Commendation. Presented USMC CI Teams ongoing technical briefings/technical support during field exercises. Provided technical operational support to Director of Intelligence, HQMC. 1984-90: established Foreign Material Exploitation (FME) Unit at Quantico to exploit hostile material on the battlefield for USMC ground commanders. Ongoing briefings to CG FMFLANT re technical state-of-the-art; G-2 II MAF re FME Unit support to II MAF; and CG/G-4 II FSSG re FME exploitation support during hostilities. FME

Unit exploited Soviet/Warsaw Pact material for USMC and National Intelligence Community in/outCONUS. Retired July 1991.

Joined Naval Intelligence 1968-88: technical, counter-intelligence and foreign material collections agent. Provided support to USN/USMC commands and collected foreign intelligence throughout Europe, Africa and Near East. Letter of Commendation (CTF-157); Certificate (Commanding General, Berlin Brigade). Headed foreign intelligence collection operations; member, working HUMINT, Counter-Terrorism, Technology Transfer Sub-Committees, US Intelligence Board; headed security for US Senate Delegations outCONUS; headed special operations outCONUS. Letter of appreciation (William S. Cohen, US Senator); Tribute of Appreciation (George Shultz, Secretary of State).

St. John's University: BA/attended Law School; BSEE (CIT); Master Certificate (American University).

Married Mary O'Donnell and has two daughters and three grandchildren.

CHARLES W. "CHUCK" COUCH, Lieutenant Colonel, born Jan. 8, 1938 in Ashland, KS. Trained 1960-62, Pensacola, FL and Beeville, TX. Served with VMF-333, MCAS Beaufort, MARTD Olathe, MARTD Los Alamitos, MARTD EL Toro. Left the service in 1978 and is now a rancher.

JAMES A. "JIM" CRAIGE, Lieutenant Colonel, born June 7, 1931 in Lansing, MI. Enlisted as private in USMCR in 1948, Atlanta, GA; Boot Camp, 1950, Parris Island, SC; 1957: OCS, Quantico, Basic School; Comm. School, 1960, served with 1st MarDiv., 2nd MarDiv. 3rd MarDiv., US Naval Security Group, Kami Seya Japan, 1960-62; HQMC: Staff Officer Group

Div., 1966-69; USMCR 1948-62; USMC 1962-69; USMCR 1970-82.

Active duty includes: 1950-52, 2nd MarDiv. Infantry; served as Infantry Officer, 1st, 2nd, 3rd MarDiv.; 1957-69, Advisor 1st ARVN Div., RVN, 1964-65; Attended Reserve Staff Courses, Quantico, MCCAS 1975.

Military awards include the Bronze Star w/Combat V; Combat Action Ribbon; USMCR Ribbon and other campaign medals.

He is retired from US Dept. of Energy, Washington, DC and is currently a volunteer with the Colorado Springs Police Department.

He and his wife, Earlene, have three children: James (police officer), Christopher (Capt., USAF) and daughter, Tracy (lawyer).

DANIEL L. CRIPE, Colonel, born Dec. 14, 1942 in Los Angeles, CA. Enlisted USMCR January 1965; Boot Camp at MCRD, San Diego, CA.; OCS, August 1966; MCB Quantico; commissioned 2nd lieutenant, September 1966. TBS 3-67, flight schools at NAS Pensacola and NAF Glynco, earning RIO wings, March 1968.

Served with VMFA-251, MCAS Beaufort. Reported to Vietnam October 1968, in combat with VMFA-115, MAG-13, Chu Lai RVN, October 1968-November 1969. Flew over 400 F-4 Phantom combat sorties with the "Screaming Eagles." Awarded DFC, 26 Air Medals (two single mission awards), Navy Commendation w/V and other campaign medals/ribbons. Flew in combat with Maj. Adonn Sloan and Capt. Mike Wholley. 1st. Lt. Thomas Reich, lost to enemy fire, but remembered.

To CONUS November 1969, serving with MAG-13, MCAS, El Toro until release from active duty March 1971. Joined 4th Div., USMCR, 1973-94. Served with 4th ANGLICO, 3rd Bn.,

23rd Marines, Beach and Port Operations Co, San Jose, CA, (CO 1978-79), earning Marine Parachute Wings. Joined 4th Tank Bn., San Diego, XO, 1981-83, serving with Col. Mike Eddy (CO) and CWO-4 Jim "Gunner" Carroll.

Joined 2nd MEB, G-3 Staff participating in two major reserve operations from 1984-1988. Joined 4th MEF, G-3 Staff, MCB Camp Pendleton, CA 1990-92. Recalled to active duty, January-July 1991 for Operation Desert Storm serving as G-5, 5th MEF, MCB, Camp Pendleton, January-April 1991. Ordered to Saudi Arabia as G-3, Marine Forces Southwest Asia, April-June 1991, assisting in post-operation activities, awarded MSM. Retired May 1994.

Education includes a BA, Chapman College, 1964, with graduate work at Stanford University, 1975-76. Law enforcement career 1972-2001 with US Customs Service and San Diego County Sheriff's Department.

He has two sons, Daniel and Dustin, and two daughters, Nicole and Danielle.

J. MAURICE DANTIN, Colonel, born Dec. 13, 1929 in Columbia, MS. Training: 1951, MCR Dep. PISC; 1951-52 10th SBC, MCS and C&S School, Quantico.

Served with Recon Co., HQBN 2nd MarDiv., 1952-53; VMF-124, Mps. Intel O; 1953-55, VMF-143, NOLA Intel O; 1955-58; HMR-767, NAS, NOLA, Adm. O, 1958-62; MARG-18, NOLA, S-1, 1962-70; 21st Staff Group, 4th MAW, 1970-75.

Memorable experiences and achievements being CO of 21st Staff Group; organizer and first CO of VTU-13; Organizer and First President of F. Edward Herbert Chapter (NOCA) of MCROA.

Education includes: BA and JD University of Mississippi; former mayor of Columbia, MS; former district attorney for 15th Judicial District of MS; Dem. nominee for US Senate 1978.

He is an attorney and married to Sarah Patty Ponder; they have four children and four grandchildren.

ROBERT W. "BOB" DART, CWO5, born Feb. 22, 1940 in Chicago, IL. Served with 9th Inf. Bn., MACS-22, H&HS-48, MWCS-48, MACG-48.

Military awards include: Meritorious Service Medal, Navy Commendation Medal, Navy Achievement Medal, Air Force Achievement Medal, Joint Meritorious Unit Award Ribbon, Navy Unit Citation w/Bronze Star, Marine Unit Citation w/Silver Star, Organized Marine Corps Reserve Medal w/Silver and three Bronze Stars, National Defense Service Medal w/Bronze Star, Southwest Asia Service Medal w/2 Bronze Stars, Military Outstanding Volunteer Service Medal, Artic Service Ribbon, Navy and Marine Corps Overseas Service Ribbon, Recruiting Ribbon, Armed Forces Reserve Medal w/M Device and Gold Hourglass, Kuwait Liberation Medal w/Palm Tree, Kuwait Liberation Medal (K).

Retired as commander from the Chicago Police Dept.; general manager, Chicago Transit Authority.

He is married to Eleanor "Ellie".

FRED DAVIDSON III, Colonel, began his naval career in 1963 at the USMC Officer's Candidate School in Quantico. Upon his commissioning, he reported to Camp Lejeune for training with continuing orders to WESTPAC.

While in Vietnam, he was assigned to the First Marine Aircraft Wing. After the completion of his various logistical and legal assignments at the group level, he was again assigned to Quantico. He was released from active duty in December 1969 and immediately affiliated with various OMCR units.

Reserve assignments included: XO, 4th Communications Support Co. (FMF) USMC advisor NAVRESREDCOM Region 13, MTU HQMC training officer, Congressional Reserve Unit and served as the State Emergency Preparedness Officer, USMC representative, Office of the Governor/State Adjutant General, state of Indiana.

In 1991 he was recalled to active duty for Operation Desert Storm and served

as XO of RTB-7. In July 1993, he retired from the USMC.

His military education includes various staff schools with both LFTC (LANT) and (PAC), the Amph. Warfare School, Command and Staff College and the Armed Forces Staff College.

As a civilian, he held several senior positions in private industry, was elected to public office and served in the administration of Presidents Kennedy and Johnson as a White House intern and President Regan as the Deputy Assistant Navy Secretary (RA). In 1985, he was granted knighthood in Oslo, Norway. Additionally, he was awarded the Distinguished Civilian Service Award, SECNAV, Meritorious Public Service Award USCG and received a letter of appreciation, Office of the Secretary of Defense RFPB. He was elected as a trustee of the US Naval Academy Foundation and enshrined in the MPMA Hall of Fame and appointed to the National Advisory Council of the US Navy League.

JAMES L. DAVIS, CWO4, born Dec. 14, 1934 in Baltimore, MD. Enlisted in the USMCR, 9th Rifle Co, Fort Wayne, IN while still attending college in 1954. Returned to his native Baltimore to work in his stepfather's business and transferred to the 1st Engr. Bn. (later became the 4th Cbt. Engr. Bn., 4th MarDiv.). Served as company commander, H&S Co., 1973-75; while serving with the 4th Cbt. Engr. Bn., he was employed by the state of Maryland, Dept. of General Services, Office of Real Estate; spent his last five years in state service with the Judiciary of Maryland, District Court of Maryland as asst. chief clerk of facilities until his retirement in 1994.

He continued his association with the Marine Corps affiliating with HQ Det 3, 2nd MAB; HQ Det 3, 4th MarDiv.; HQ Det 3, 4th FSSG at Anacostia, MD; Security Branch RAU, HQMC, Washington, DC;

Warfighting Center RAU, Quantico, VA and two tours with MCCDC IMA Det, Quantico, VA. He attended staff courses at Quantico and Coronado. Also completing AWS and Reserve Command and Staff Phases I and II.

He has served both in the Marine Corps League and MCROA. Having completed most of the offices he has served as Commandant of the Baltimore Chapter of the MCL and in 1979 he served as president of the Baltimore Chapter of MCROA. In 1990 he participated in Operation Desert Shield/Storm as a casualty assistant officer. Retiring from the USMCR Nov. 1, 1994 after 40 years of service.

His education includes a BS from the University of Baltimore in business management and various courses and seminars. He is married with three daughters. Presently, he is working part time as a management consultant and enjoying retirement and travel.

MICHAEL "MIKE" DECICCO, Captain, born Dec. 10, 1964 in Brooklyn, NY. Enlisted in Reserves while in college. Training: Parris Island, May-August 1985. Active Duty: OCS, February-April 1987; TBS, April-November 1987. OCS-TBS, February-October 1987; Armor School, Fort Knox, November 1987-March 1988. Served with C Co., 2nd Tank Bn., Camp Lejeune, March 1988-June 1990; B Co., 8th Tank Bn., Syracuse, NY, June 1990; Armor Assault Bn., Mount Fuji, Japan.

Memorable experiences and achievements include serving with B-Co, 8th Tank Bn. during Desert Storm.

Military Awards: Navy Achievement, Sea Service Deployment, Southwest Asia, Combat Action, National Defense, Kuwait Liberation. Capt. De Cicco retired Jan. 1, 1998.

Education: master degree in human organization science, criminal justice, Villanova University, 1993. In December 1993, he was hired by the US Secret Service and stationed in Philiadelphia, PA; 1997-present, Atlantic City Resident Office.

He and his wife, Arleen, have one daughter, Allison (b. Aug. 3, 1998).

ANDREW C. "ANDY" DELGADO, Captain, born June 17, 1954 in Hartford, CT. Training: 1st MarDiv., Camp Pendleton, CA; Jungle Operations Training Center, Fort Sherman, Panama Canal Zone, March 1978; Diver Second Class School, Naval Station, San Diego, CA, May 1978; Airborne Course, Fort Benning, GA, July 1978; 3rd MarDiv., Okinawa, Japan, October 1979-August 1980.

Units served with include I Co, 3rd Bn., 7th Marines, January 1977-January 1978; C Co, 1st Recon Bn., February 1978-August 1979; Deep Recon Plt., 3rd Recon Bn., October 1979-August 1980; A Co, 4th Tank Bn., March 1981-January 1983

Memorable experiences and achievements include participation in the rescue/safeguarding of 43 Vietnamese boat people in November 1979 while aboard the USS *Juneau* in the South China Sea. He received the Humanitarian Service Medal.

Until March 8, 1983, he worked as a master schedules administrator at Rohr Industries in Chula Vista, CA. After March 8, 1983, he was permanently handicapped as a result of being broadsided by an underage drinker who ran a stop sign.

He is married to Sharon L. Brasche and they have two sons: Anthony (killed in above mentioned auto accident) and Michael.

TERRY L. DELONG, Colonel, born March 16, 1942 in Allentown, PA. Training: PLC Program Quantico, Command and Staff School, Amph. Planning, Officers Communications School.

Served with 2nd, 5th and 9th Marines (Active Duty); Arty. Bn., Philadelphia, PA; 4th Svc. Bn., Freemansburg, PA; MACS, Denver, CO; 2nd MAB, Encino, CA, Marine Reserves.

Memorable experiences and achievements include tour in Vietnam; being member of 3/9; being in last battalion to train as a battalion (2/5 Camp Pendleton) and going over on ships as a battalion. Billet was rifle platoon commander.

His military awards include the Navy Commendation Medal w/Combat V, Presidential Unit Citation, various Vietnam Campaign Medals, MC Reserve Ribbon, National Defense. Col. DeLong retired in 1992.

Attended Princeton University for BA in economics, 1964; Drexel University, MBA in finance, 1973.

Currently he is vice president for an investment firm. He has been married to Peggy for 32 years and they have two children, Michael and Bergen, living and working in the Denver Metro area.

GUIDO DEVINCENZI, Lieutenant Colonel, born Jan. 6, 1922 in San Francisco, CA. Training: San Diego and Quantico VA. Served with 1st MarDiv., Pacific Cape Gloucester, Peleliu, Okinawa, Tientsin, Peiping, China. Served a total of 21-1/2 years Active and Reserve duty.

Memorable experiences and achievements include landing on Peleliu and Okinawa; prior to Quantico served in the enlisted ranks, attained sergeant rank after training, Base Depot, San Diego MCB.

He was recommended for Bronze Star by Col. John Raluf, Peleliu, but it never reached him or was awarded.

Currently retired after 34 years with AAA Club and Insurance.

LAWRENCE E. DICKERSON, Colonel, born July 17, 1931 in Oak Hill, WV. Served with the 1st MarDiv. in Korea as a staff sergeant prior to being commissioned in 1952. He subsequently was a platoon leader in 2nd Bn., 8th Marines and a company commander in the 1st Inf. Trng. Regt.

After release to inactive duty, he graduated from Northwestern University and served as a company commander in 2nd Bn., 24th Marines; in ANGLICO, 5th Comm. Bn. and in the 18th Staff Group.

He was president of Chicago Chapter, MCROA in 1972. He retired from Lockheed Martin Corporation, where he was manager of new employee management in 1997. He is a USA Track and Field age-group All American.

He and his wife, Charlotte, have three children and four grandchildren.

MICHAEL G. DICKERSON, Colonel, born April 15, 1938 in Chicago, IL. Commissioned as a regular NROTC Midshipman at Yale University in 1956, he graduated in 1960 and was commissioned a 2nd lieutenant in the USMC 3-60 Basic Class, Quantico, preflight and basic flight training, Pensacola, jet advanced flight training, Kingsville, TX, designated naval aviator #18779 on May 25, 1962. 1st Squadron was VMA-212 MCAS Kaneoha Bay, Oahu (A-4s).

Transitioned to F-8 Crusaders (VMF-212). Forward Air Controller, 1st Anglico at Camp Smith, Hawaii. Joined MAG-11 at Atsugi, Japan in July 1965 and immediately deployed to Da Nang, Vietnam. No F-8s in MAG-11 initially, so 1st Air Medal was awarded for flying Air Force U-10 propaganda missions in I Corps. Joined VMA 214 Blacksheep at Iwakuni in April 1966 and returned with them to Chu Lai. Graduated from Amph. Warfare School, January 1967. Combat Replacement Pilot Instructor VMT 103, Yuma, AZ, April 1967-September 1968. MAG-12 Chu Lai, Vietnam, September 1968-October 1969.

Final combat tally, 400 missions, 24 Air Medals.

Transferred to USMCR, December 1969 and retired from the active reserves in 1983. After active duty (1969) he joined the investment banking firm of Kidder Peabody in New York, becoming a shareholder/partner in 1975 and retired in 1993. Chairman/CEO, Neptune Interactive Communications, Alexandria, VA, 1996. Consultant to NCT Group, 1993 to present.

Recollections/Acknowledgment: Lt. Joe Kerwin was Dickerson's preflight class leader. He was a flight surgeon/naval aviator, who in 1961 wanted to become the first doctor in space, was the ground capsule coordinator welcoming Apollo 13 back to earth and went on to achieve his goal

by performing a space walk on a shuttle mission to free a solar panel.

Col. Dooley, Hawaiian Marine Air Group Commander, got them carqualed on every carrier that he could. A real challenge for the junior squadron pilot (Dickerson).

Dave Lerps was his first LSO and witnessed Dickerson's night IFR carrier catapult launch off of Oahu before he had ever made a night VFR landing or launch.

Major Tom Hagen (VMA-214 Blacksheep Executive Officer) made Dickerson's first real combat flying possible by letting him "refam" in the A-4 at Iwakuni in March 1966.

Col. Rex. A. Deasy, VMT 103 Sqdn. CO and then MAG 12 CO for his second tour in Vietnam, is a treasured mentor.

Then Lt. (flight surgeon) and now Adm. Jim Fowler, who almost had to eject because Dickerson overextended the range of a TA-4 on a hop out of Yuma, AZ.

LtCol. Warfield, who saved Dickerson's butt when he had a full electrical failure, by leading him back to Chu Lai in IFR conditions on his wing and then through a last minute wave off/go-round because of another aircraft on the runway.

Dave Sites, who remembered what to do with the emergency fuel tank transfer in the TA-4 when Dickerson suggested that they make a "Mayday" call over North Vietnam.

Tony Miller, a squadron mate, who was truly the "Cat with nine lives."

Roy Stocking for the "hung elephants" and other stories.

Bill Williams for trusting him to be the "Top Gun" at the Pendleton exercises in 1970. And finally, because they never forget their boot camp experiences, DI/LCpl. Gross and 2nd Lt. Phil Christ.

GEORGE K. DIKE, Colonel, born April 6, 1918 in Grafton, ND. Training: 5th OCC, January 1942; Quantico, VA, 1942; 1943, New River, NC; 1944, Fort Sill, OK; Camp Pendleton, CA; Camp Tarawa, HI.

Served with 51st Composite Defense Bn.; J Btry, 3rd Bn.; 5th MarDiv.; enlisted MCR, May 7, 1941, commissioned April 4, 1942; AD Jan. 30, 1942-Feb. 18, 1946 to Captain; AD

Aug. 17, 1950-May 15, 1955 to lieutenant colonel. Retired 1976, COL, USMCR.

Memorable experiences and achievements include serving with first African-American unit in USMC, 1942; landing on Iwo Jima, 1945; occupation duty, Japan, 1945.

His military awards include the Purple Heart and Bronze Star w/Combat V.

He has a PHD degree from Michigan State University, 1961 and is now a retired faculty member from Michigan State University. He is married with six children.

DONALD GENE "DON" DIXON, CWO4, born June 13, 1936 in Lenoxburg, KY. Trained 1952, PISC; 1963 Quantico, VA. Served with 1st MarDiv.; 2nd MarDiv.; 3rd Marine Airwing and 4th MarDiv.

Memorable experiences and achievements include serving as president of MCROA local chapter; elected as detachment and state MCL commandant; being selected for WO with 10 years of service in USMC.

He received the Meritorious Service Medal; Korean Service Medal, Good Conduct Medal w/star and National Defense Service Medal w/star.

He and his wife, Effie, have four children.

HUGH L. "LARRY" DOUGHERTY JR., Colonel, born April 15, 1932 in Norfolk, VA. In 1954 he graduated from Virginia Military Institute (VMI) and was commissioned a 2nd lieutenant in the USMC. In December of 1954, following graduation from Officer Basic School, Quantico, VA, he was issued orders to the 1st MarDiv. in Korea but was retained at Camp Pendleton, CA to form a cadre for 1st MarDiv. returning to CONIUS. He was assigned to the 1st Pioneer Bn. and assisted in the rebuilding of the engineering assests of the 1st MarDiv.

In 1956 he received orders to Supply School at Camp Lejeune, NC which was followed by an assignment as Marine Corps Supply Officer, MAG-16, 1st MAW in Oppama, Japan. To complete a two year tour in supply, he was assigned to the 2nd Force Service Regt., 2nd MarDiv., Morehead City, NC for the Lebanon crisis in 1958.

Then they returned to CONUS and were sent to the Advanced Engineer Officers School at Fort Belvoir, VA; back to the 1st Engr. Bn., 1st MarDiv., Camp Pendleton, CA. He served as CO, B Co., 1st Engr. Bn. and as S-4 Logistics Officer before being assigned as I&I, 4th Engr. Co., Charleston, WV. In 1963 he requested and received orders to the USMCR and settled in Norfolk and Virginia Beach, VA.

He remained in the reserve program serving in various staff and command positions with the Supply Bn., Norfolk and then with a VTU assigned to CG, FMFLANT, Norfolk completing 30 years of service.

His civilian career was as a banking official for approximately 15 years and as the CEO of a subsidiary corporation involved in real estate, development and construction, mortgage banking, general insurance and real estate appraisal.

JAMES W. "JIM" DUKE, Lieutenant Colonel, born Feb. 27, 1929 in Olla, LA. Trained at Parris Island, 1951; Quantico, VA, 1951-52. Served with: 3rd Sig. Bn.; 3rd MarDiv.; VMF-143; MACS-18; MASS-4; MAG-46; 4th Marines Regt; VTU - Alameda, CA; VTU - Sacramento, CA.

He is a retired college president and has a BA and MA from LSU and a doctorate degree from USC. He is married to Betty Olsen and they have two sons and two daughters.

MONTE E. DUNARD, Lieutenant Colonel, born Nov. 18, 1957 in Troy, MO. Training: TBS, Quantico, VA; FLT School, Pensacola, FL; Tustin, CA, CH-46s.

He served with HMM-164, 3rd MAW, Tustin, CA, HMM-764, 4th MAW, El Toro, CA; 4th MAW HQ, New Orleans, LA.

Memorable experiences and achievements include Flying Toys for Tots Christmas 1996 and 1998; mission to Grand Canyon with three CH-46s; being activated for Desert Shield/Storm.

He is currently a pilot for American Airlines. He and his wife, Cindy, have one son, Nicholas.

MICHAEL C. "MIKE" EDDINGS, Major, born Jan. 2, 1945 in Houston, TX. Training: May 1971 OCS, Quantico, VA; TBS, Quantico, VA, Naval Flight Training; NAS, Pensacola, FL.

Units served with: HMH-461, HMH-777, HMH-772, Det-B, MABS, MCAS, New River, NC; 1st Bn., 23rd Marines, Houston, TX.

Memorable experiences and achievements include flying first night landing missions with night vision goggles with HMH-461 in 1973-74; being selected to evaluate flight simulator training in H-53 for USMC.

He is currently an attorney. Married Shirley on Aug. 23, 1963 and they have one son, Michael, and one daughter, Michele.

RANDALL E. "RANDY" EGERTSON, Colonel, born Sept. 15, 1933 in Minneapolis, MN. Training: Basic School, Quantico, VA, March 1955; Flight School, Pensacola, 1956-57.

He was commissioned through NROTC at Oregon State University in 1955, BSME, and served with HMR-361, H&MS-36, HMM-770, HMM-764, H&MS-46 (MAG-46 Staff).

Memorable experiences and achievements include serving with HMR-361 on Operation Hardinek (atomic testing at Bikini Atoll - 1958), also served as deputy commander, MAG-46 from 1979-83.

Military Awards include Meritorious Service Medal and Marine Corps Reserve Medal.

He is a retired consulting engineer. He and his wife, Diane, have two sons and three grandchildren.

KEN A. ELMENDORF, Colonel, was commissioned as 2nd lieutenant from OCS in 1966. In 1967, after completing Tracked Vehicle School, he reported to

the 3rd AMTRAC Bn. in Vietnam where he served as a platoon commander.

Upon his return from Vietnam, he served as an economics instructor at the US Naval Academy until June of 1970 when he was released from active duty. He joined the reserves in Indianapolis and from 1975 until 1978 served a CO, Comm. Spt. Co. The next two years he served with the 1st Bn., 24th Marines, Detroit, MI.

Following a tour with MCMS, Cincinnati, OH, he joined HQ, Det. 4, Chicago, IL where he served until 1983. He then became CO, MWCS-48, Glenview. In 1985 he returned to active duty for one year as an Econ Instructor at the USNA. In 1986 he became executive officer, MSWSG-47, Selfridge. The next duty was for two years as OIC, MCMS, Louisville, KY.

In 1991 he was recalled to active duty during Operation Desert Storm as OIC, 6th Mobilization Region, Overland Park. He completed his career as the Marine Corps Liaison Officer, Naval Reserve Readiness Command Region 13, Great Lakes.

Throughout his distinguished career, he earned numerous personal awards which include; Bronze Star w/ Combat V (two awards), Purple Heart, Navy and Marine Corps Commendation Medal (two awards), Combat Action Ribbon, PUC, NUC, MUC and Vietnamese Cross of Gallantry.

He held a BS in mathematics and physics, MA in economics from Ball State University. He held a doctor of jurisprudence from Indiana University Law School. In civilian life he practiced law in Brownsburg, IN and was a professor of business at Marian College in Indianapolis, IN.

There was not a day the he was not seen with a smile on his face and story to tell you. As a ventriloquist with his sidekick Elmer entertainment was his great delight. He and Elmer were together in Vietnam, USNA and numerous Corps and friends events.

Col. Elmendorf died on Jan. 8, 1999 of a heart attack and was buried in Arlington National Cemetery on Jan. 20, 1999. He is survived by his wife, NJ, and their children: Brett, Dirk and Beth.

JUNIOR HENRY "HANK" ENNEN, Colonel, born Feb. 15, 1920 in Lincoln, NE. Entered service April 14, 1942 in the V5 program, Long Beach, CA. Commissioned 2nd Lt. USMCR, February 1943, Corpus Christi, TX. Ordered overseas in March 1943. Served with VMSB-3, VMTB-131, VMF-312.

During the battle of Peleliu and Okinawa, flew 162 combat missions WWII. Returned from overseas December 1945 and joined MCR, Sqdn. VMF-123 at Los Alamitos, CA.

He was a coach and associate athletic director for California State University in Los Angeles, CA until called up for duty in Korea with MAG-33 in 1951.

He returned to CONUS in 1953 and again joined the squadron at Los Alamitos, CA, JMF-123. He served as CO of MASS-4, CO and EX of MARG II, 1958-64. CO of MARTCOM Liaison Advanced Party at Cherry Point, NC, El Toro, CA and Yuma, AZ during summer reserve training.

In 1965 was awarded a SWAG contract with the reserve program in Quantico, VA as head of the reserve branch until 1969, then he was transferred to the Pentagon, Office of the Asst. Sec. of Defense (Reserve Affairs) as head of the facilities and logistics branch. He was the first Marine officer assigned to this billet. He retired in 1974 from the Pentagon.

His education includes BA from UCLA, MA from California State University at Los Angeles.

Some of his memorable experiences include: 1970 assisted in the original writing and development of the *Total Force Concept* for reserve forces.

His military awards include: LOM, Naval Commendation Medal, JSM, AM w/Gold Star and other campaign and commendation awards.

He is married to the former Maxine Carlton of Long Beach, CA and they have four children: Jeff, Connie, John and Sharron.

PAUL GERIN "SPIKE" FAHLSTROM, Colonel, born May 15, 1929 in Colquet, MN. Training: 1949-50, 1953, Quantico VA; 1954-55, Pensacola, FL.

Served with VMA-323, VMA-321, MTU MD-4.

He is a retired aero engineer and is married with three children.

KEITH G. FELIX, Colonel, born March 8, 1918 in Tippecanoe County, IN. Graduated Purdue University, 1942. Enlisted Officers Candidate Class, Oct. 17, 1942. Boot Camp, Parris Island, SC, 1942-43. OCC at Quantico and commissioned 2nd Lt. April 1943, followed by 25th Reserve Officers Class, 1943-44 and attended Naval Communications School at Harvard University. Then to Army Officers Communication School, Fort Benning, GA.

He left San Diego for Pearl Harbor, Sept. 16, 1944 by ship and flew from there to Guadalcanal to join the 6th Joint Assault Signal Co., 6th MarDiv as Comm. Officer. He participated in Battle of Okinawa, landing with assault waves April 1, 1945. In July 1945 he left Okinawa for Guam to train for anticipated invasion of Japan. After the Japanese surrender August 1945, he went with 6th MarDiv. from Guam to Tsingtao, China as CO of 6th JAS Co. There he participated in surrender of Japanese troops in Tsingtao area.

Returned to CONUS, Jan. 29, 1946 and released to inactive duty April 1946. He was a member of the Volunteer Training Unit 9-5, South Bend, IN from 1950-62. He attended MC Staff College at Quantico Naval War College and various other military schools.

In July 1962 he organized the 6th Engr. Bn., USMCR, FMF with headquarters at South Bend, IN. He served as CO from 1962-66 and then organized an Engineer Volunteer Training Unit at South Bend. In 1973, he was elected president of Reserve Officers Assn. of the US, Department of Indiana, serving until 1974.

He did graduate studies at Purdue University in 1946. He organized Felix

& Associates, Inc. at Plymouth, IN, a real estate sales and development company and insurance agency, serving as president until he retired in 1983.

Married Arline C. Hickisch and they have one daughter, Patricia; two sons, Keith II and Kevin; and six grandsons.

LEWIS C. FERRETTI, Colonel, born Jan. 30, 1932 in Cape Cod, MA. Commissioned from the 8th OCC, he completed the 26th SBC and was assigned to Marine Air Control Sqdn. 1, 1st MAW, FMF, in Korea, for duties as machine gun platoon commander, air defense control officer, then as squadron S-3.

Returning to CONUS, he was RELFRACDU and assigned to MACS-21, NAS, South Weymouth; then MACS-15, NAS, Atlanta; 5th Comm Co, ForTrps, FMF and 10th Staff Group (Ground), Greensboro, NC. His duties included AirDefContO, CommO, Radio Plt Cmdr, RadarO and Comm&ElectO.

In Greensboro, he was CO of Comm Co. H&S Bn., 4th FSR, ForTrps, FMF; VTU 6-3; MTU NC02; and MTU (INT) NC02. MTU (INT) NCO2 was under permanent operational control of CG, MCDEC to support the intelligence division of the Development Center with development of texts, programs of instruction and investigation of intelligence processing systems.

He attended AWS, CommO School and C&S College, Quantico; Landing Force Staff and Air Ground Task Force Planning courses at Coronado and Little Creek; and was a student and then a moderator at National Defense University, Washington, DC.

His awards include NDSM, KCSM, UNKSM, two Organized Marine Corps Reserve Medals, Armed Forces Reserve-Marine Corps Medal. Col. Ferretti retired in 1984.

A member of MCROA since 1957, he was on the board of directors as 6th district director in 1970-71 and a member of the executive council in 1972-74 and 1978-79.

His education includes a BS from Providence College and MBA from Boston College. He has held financial, administrative and operational management positions with several corporations and in 1989, retired as president & CEO of The Alderman Co., High Point, NC. He is presently owner of Lewis C. Ferretti & Associates-Insurance & Financial Services in NC and New England. He and his wife, Helen, have four sons and 10 grandchildren.

PETER J. FINLEY, Colonel, born Sept. 9, 1931 in Philadelphia, PA. He was sworn into the Marine Crops on Jan. 25, 1955, completed the 14th OCC and was commissioned a 2nd Lt. on Dec. 15, 1955 and graduated with the I-56 OBC. His first assignment was as platoon commander with 3/2/2.

He deployed to the Mediterranean Sea and participated in the evacuation of the UN truce team and American Nationals from Gaza, Israel and Alexandria, Egypt. Naval gunline spotter, embarkation and custodian of classified documents schools followed assignment to 2/2/2. Golf Co, 2/2 deployed to the Mediterranean Sea in May 1958 as company executive offers. He participated in the Marine landing at Beirut, Lebanon on July 15, 1958 and received a personal commendation for that operation.

After release from active duty, he served in the Organized Marine Corps Reserve program with the 69th Rife Co, MAG-42, later as CO of VTU-24 and the Marine Corps Reserve Mobilization Station, Philadelphia, PA.

In July 1966, he began duty as a Special Project Officer at HQMC with assignments that included: establishing the special training branch, MCRD, PISO; Project 100,000; Project Transition; reorganization of the correctional system; modifying officer and enlisted recruitment standards; the training of recruiters and OSOs; evaluation procedures of OBC and WOBC and AWS programs of instruction; establishing the Worldwide Family Service Centers and a detachment

commanders attrition study for MSG Bn. Additionally, in 1982 he was assigned to, and, contributed to the development of the Reserve Special Staff Officers program as the 4th Marine Corps District Coordinator and later as national coordinator from 1984-86. He retired on June 30, 1986 and in March 1987 was recalled to active duty to establish a program of psychological services for the Marine Security Guard Bn., the Marine Corps Presidential Support Program (Yonker White) and for HMX-1.

After his return to retired status, he served as the psychology consultant to MSG Bn. until September 1995 and the Presidential Support/HMX-1 programs until September 1998. He as awarded the LOM and recommended for the Presidential Service Badge.

He hold a BA in psychology from La Salle University; an MS in clinical psychology from the College of William and Mary and a doctorate in school psychology from Temple University.

He is married to Anne Maron Ryan and they have five children: Peter, Kathleen, Anne, Patrick and Matthew.

DANIEL ROSS "DAN" FOLEY, Colonel, born Nov. 11, 1938 in Kansas City, MO. Graduated Rockhurst College, Kansas City and conducted graduate studies at California State University, Los Angeles. He performed enlisted service in the USN and was commissioned in the USMCR in 1970. His military career has been about equally divided among tactical, national and joint intelligence assignments.

He has served as an assistant S-2, counterintelligence team commander, joint intelligence center order of battle officer, intelligence watch officer, watch commander, area analyst and warning officer. Following recall to active duty for Desert Storm, he served

on extended active duty assignments to the director of Central Intelligence, National Intelligence Officer for Warning; J2, National Military Joint Intelligence Center (NMJIC); and HQMC as the Intelligence Division (C41) action officer for development of the USMCR Intelligence Program. From 1993-96, he was the OIC of the HQMC Intelligence IMA Detachment which support the NMJIC as well as other organizations of the National Intelligence Community. He assumed command of the J2 Joint Reserve Intelligence Unit, Defense Intelligence Agency (DIA), Washington, DC on Sept. 14, 1996 and retired on June 6, 1998.

He pursued a civilian career in federal law enforcement and was employed first as a special agent of the Naval Investigative Service and then the Office of Inspector General, Department of Defense. He was a member of the Federal Senior Executive Service and served as acting assistant inspector general for Criminal Investigations Policy and Oversight and deputy director, Defense Criminal Investigative Service.

His personal decorations include: LOM, Defense Meritorious Service Medal w/OLC, MSM, JSCM, Navy Good Conduct Medal and the Joint Chiefs of Staff Identification Badge.

He reside in Williamsburg, VA with his wife, the former Imelda Charay of Kansas City, MO. They have three children: Sara, Karrie and Daniel; and granddaughter, Heather Marie.

THEODORE C. "TED" FOSS, Major, born December 1936 in Seattle, WA. Trained: PLC, 1956, 1958, Quantico, VA; 3-59 Basic School Class, Quantico, VA.

Served with: April 1955-July 1950, VMF-216 (Reserve) NAS, Seattle, WA;

June 1960-July 1961, M Battery, 4-12, Third MarDiv (FMF)(REINF); August 1961-April 1963, SMS, MCAS, El Toro, CA; May 1963-April 1973 VMR-353 (Reserve) NAS, Seattle, WA; May 1973-April 1977, VTU-2 (AVN) NS, Seattle, WA. Maj. Foss retired in December 1996.

Memorable experience was meeting the Queen Mother of United Kingdom in 1973.

He has BA from the University of Washington, 1959 and M.Ed from the University of Washington, 1967. He retired after 35 years as a Washington State educator.

He is a lifetime member of MCROA, Seattle Chapter. Fulbright Educator to London, UK, 1972-73. Counselor with AIFS, 1980, 1985. Member of Phi Delta Kappa, Educ. Honorary.

He and his wife, Maxine, have one son, Daniel (1996 Summer Olympics torch relay runner), and two daughters, Kathryn and Karen.

GEORGE R. "MADDAWG" FRANCIS JR, CWO4, USMCR, born

in Harnett County, NC. Joined USMC Nov. 28, 1960; recruit training, Parris Island; ITR, Camp Geiger; Field Artillery School, Fort Sill, OK; assigned to the 2nd Field Artillery Group, Camp Lejeune.

After active duty, joined the 4th 155 Howitzer Battery USMCR unit in Raleigh, NC. Became the youngest GySgt. in the USMCR. Later served with the Richmond, VA 105 Howitzer Battery. Ran and finished the very first Marine Corps Marathon in 1976. Joined Alpha Co., 8th Tank Bn., Louisville/Fort Knox, KY in 1979. Promoted to 1st. Sgt. in 1980. Served as Company 1st Sgt. of Alpha Co., 8th Tanks through September 1981, when selected for the warrant officer program.

Summer of 1982, attended Warrant Officer School, Quantico, VA, graduating 16th in his class. Served as a platoon leader with 8th Tanks at Fort Knox; joined Lima Battery, 4/14, Bessemer, AL, as safety officer and NBC officer. In 1986, joined the 4th FSSG, Atlanta, GA, as the historical officer, was selected for

the Defense Information School at Fort Benjamin Harrison and completed the Public Affairs Officer Course. In 1988, became the group public affairs officer of the 4th FSSG under command of BGen. Joe Wilson. Awarded Navy Achievement (2) and the Navy and Marine Corps Commendation.

In October 1990, rejoined the primary staff of BGen. Wilson as the pubic affairs officer of the 2nd MEB, Camp Lejeune. Was called to active duty Dec. 1, 1990, in support of Desert Shield/Storm. Dec. 15, 1990, joined the IIMEF pubic affairs staff in SWA as a media escort officer. Returned to CONUS, February 1991, to rejoin 2nd MEB as it was being activated. Deployed with 2nd MEB to Norway for first full execution of the NALMEB concept during Battle Griffin 91. Released from active duty, May 1991.

Summer of 1991, served on MajGen. Mitch Waters' select committee to commemorate the 75th anniversary of the Marine Corps Reserve at HQMC. Returned to Norway with 2nd MEB for Battle Griffin 93.

He is currently serving in the IRR and plans to retire, after 40 years of service, in the year 2000. Francis is a life member of MCROA, the Once a Marine Society, VFW and the American Legion.

Education includes studies at East Carolina University, first as a music major and then as a political science and economics major. Additional studies at North Carolina State University, the University of Louisville and business seminars at the University of North Carolina at Chapel Hill and at Harvard.

Currently he is serving as chairman of the board of AmCom General Corporation.

He has two sons, two daughters and one granddaughter and lives in Seneca, SC.

FRANK G. FRANKOSKY, Captain,

born Jan. 9, 1920 in Billings, MT. Trained; 1942, University of Iowa, Preflight; 1943,

Wold Chamberland Field, Primary -1943; August 1943 received wings at Pensacola Air Station.

Served with VMR-953 in Pacific.

Award received: Squadron – Presidential Citation for carrying most freight of any marine transport squadron in Pacific without casualties, 1944-45.

He graduated with honors (civil engineering) from University of Minnesota and was president of a large engineering consulting firm until retirement.

He and his wife, Doris, have five children and 12 grandchildren.

ROBERT DOUGLAS "ROB" FREEMAN, XO, born June 26, 1967

in Washington, DC. Trained PLC/OCS Jr. Camp Upshur, 1987; PLC/OCS Sr. Brown Field, 1988; TBS C Co, 1990.

Units Served with: HQ Co 8th Marines, supply officer, November 1990-June 1991; 2/4, supply officer, June 1991-November 1992; HQ Bn. 2nd MarDiv., asst. supply officer, November 1992-September 1993; Supply Co. 4th Spt. Bn., 4th FSSG, plt. comdr., trng. officer, February 1994-July 1997; Ration Co. 4th Spt. Bn., 4th FSSG, XO, July 1997-present.

Memorable experiences and achievements include Desert Shield/Desert Storm; Mediterranean deployment shortly after outbreak of Croatian Civil War w/BLT 2/4, 24th MEU (SOC); deployment to Mountain Warfare Training Center. Completed Amphibious Warfare School in 1995. Currently working towards MBA.

Military Awards include ARCOM, Navy Achievement Medal, Combat Action Ribbon, Navy Unit Commendation, Selected Marine Corps Reserve Medal, NDSM, SWA Service Medal w/ 3 Bronze Stars, Military Outstanding Volunteer Service Medal, Sea Service Deployment Ribbon w/Bronze Star, Kuwaiti Liberation Medal (Saudi Government), Kuwaiti Liberation Medal (Kuwaiti Government).

He is employed as a program analysts by CALIBRE Systems, Inc. for past five years, conducting commercial activities studies for A-76 programs at various military installations, and development of annual operating and support cost reports for Army and Marine Corps major end items.

He and his wife, Vi, have one son, Sean Robert.

PATRICK W. FULLER, Colonel, born Oct. 27, 1918 in Seymour, WS. Trained: Quantico, VA, Artillery in Camp Lejeune, NC. Served with the 12th Defense Bn.

While in the Reserves he wrote the manual and organized the Devil Pups Program, centered in the Los Angeles area, 1963 until the present.

He was the chief inspector of DEA until retirement in 1975. He and his wife, Virginia, have one daughter, Gay Parkinson, of Wellsville, UT.

JEROME M. "JERRY" GARDBERG, Lieutenant Colonel, born Dec. 27, 1936 in Atlanta, GA. He enlisted in the 9th Inf. Bn., USMCR in Chicago in July 1954 and was commissioned in the OCC program in December 1959. He served for two years with the 3rd MarDiv. on Okinawa and Marine Range Detachment, Mt. Fuji, Japan as a communications officer.

He returned to CONUS in December 1962 and joined MACS-22, NAS, Glenview, IL and later H&HS-48, MACG-48 and served variously as CommO and AdminO. In February 1973 he was appointed XO and subsequently CO of MWCTS-407. After his graduation from law school he was designated as a trial/defense counsel. Following these billets he joined MTU-IL6 (Law) and served as AdminO and CO. He later served with the Mobilization Station in Chicago.

He was transferred to the Retired Reserves in July 1986 with nearly 32 years of service. His awards include the AFRM w/2 Hour Glass Devices, Organized Marine Corps Medal w/4 stars and the NDSM.

His education includes a BS from Roosevelt University in Chicago and a JD from Chicago-Kent College of Law (IIT). He was licensed as a certified financial planner and his career included

private law practice and trust management for commercial banks. He attended various staff courses including Amphibious Warfare School, Military Justice Course, Command and Staff Course and Reserve Components National Security Course. He is a life member of MCROA.

His many community activities include being president of northwest Indiana organizations of the Federal Bar Association, The Jewish Federation, Arts Association and Munster Rotary Club.

He and his wife, Fran, of 35 years have two girls and two boys, the oldest of whom served in the Israeli Defense Force.

WINSTON L. "GARY" GARESCHE, Captain, born June 11, 1920 in Detroit, MI. Trained: Camp Pendleton, NC, 1955-57; Camp Lejeune, NC, 1958-67, NAS JAX, 1956.

Served with: 8th Engr. Co., FMF, Orlando, FL; HMM-765 MARTD, 4th AMTRAC Bn. (Rein) FMF, Tampa, FL; VMA-341 (NAS JAX); 2nd Shore Party Group Co, Orlando, FL.

From 1941-46 served with the US Army, 1946-51 served with the USAF. In January 1955 enlisted in the USMCR. Served 27 months in Pacific Theatre. Retired June 11, 1980.

His military awards include the Army GCM, American Defense, ACM, Pacific Campaign Medal, Korean Service Medal, WWII Victory Medal and AFRM.

He retired from Chevron Chemical Co. after 29 years. He and his wife, Pat, have one son, Gary, two grandchildren and two great-grandchildren.

GREGORY KENT "GIFF" GIFFORD, Captain, born Oct. 1, 1957 in Orange, NJ. Training: TBS Charlie Co, 3-80, IOC, Pensacola, Japan, Panama, OCS, 1979.

Served with 4th Marines, 4th MAB, Fox Co., MCRD PISC, 2/235 (Fox Co).

Memorable experiences and achievements include being CO Fox Co., 2/235, the NYC Marines.

Current Profession: Technology Services/COMDISCO. He and his wife, Kimberly, reside in Geneva, IL.

PETER R. GLIGOR, Colonel, commissioned via the PLC program in June 1962 after graduating from Mount Union College in Alliance, OH. He reported to Pensacola, FL for flight training and received his naval aviator wings in January 1964.

He was then assigned to HMM-261 at MCAF, New River, NC. After extensive training the squadron was sent to the Republic of Vietnam in June 1965. He flew the H-34 for 397 combat missions in Vietnam for HMM-261 and HMM-362. He was awarded 19 Air Medals, a Presidential Unit Citation and a Navy Unit Commendation.

Returning to the US in July 1966, he was assigned adjutant of HMMT-301 and later asst. operation officer of MCAS, Santa Ana, CA.

After release from active duty and completion of TWA training, he reported to the NAS at Brooklyn, NY for duty with HMM-768.

In 1970 he transitioned to the H-46 at NAS, Lakehurst, NJ and in 1972 he began flying the H-53 at NAS, Willow Grove, PA as a member of HMM-772. Squadron billets included admin officer, asst. operations officer and executive officer. Other assignments included OIC of Marine Air Traffic Control, Unit-73 and MAG-49, S-1 officer.

In April of 1982, then LtCol. Gligor was selected to be the executive officer of the Marine Corps support detachment at Andrews AFB, Washington, DC. There he flew the Beechcraft C-12 for the commandants of the Marine Corps, John Barrow and P.X. Kelly, as well as other flag officers at HQMC and the Pentagon.

After promotion to colonel in 1984, he transferred to a mobilization training unit in New York State. Eventually becoming commanding officer. He then served as a control officer for the National Defense University at Fort McNair in Washington, DC in the war games and simulation center for several years until his retirement in 1992.

Col. Gligor and his wife, the former Marilyn Stevenson, have four children: Laura, Sharon, Gary and Brian. He is currently employed as a Boeing 767 captain for Trans World Airlines at Kennedy Airport in New York.

WILLIAM JOHN "BILL" GLYECK, Colonel, born June 24, 1941 in Cincinnati, OH. Trained at Camp Lejeune, CARIB, CamPen, Vietnam, CamPen, 4th LSB, Seattle. Units served include 3/8, 2/26, MACV 3rd Marines, Staging Bn., 4th LSB, Provisional Spt. Bn. (PAC).

During his military career he served as an infantry officer; in Vietnam as platoon commander, company executive officer, infantry battalion advisor to the Vietnamese Army, and division combat intelligence officer, Battalion Commander of 4th Landing Support Bn. and Provisional Support Bn. (Pacific), 4th Force Service Support Group, Marine Forces Reserve.

Education: Marine Corps Command and Staff College; Navy War College; National Defense University; Ohio State University, BA in economics, minor in math, 1959-64; Stanford University, MBA and JD, 1968-72.

Memorable experiences and achievements include being on top of Mt. Adams when St. Helens erupted in 1980.

Col. Glueck retired in 1995. His awards include the Bronze Star Medal w/Combat V; RVN Cross of Gallantry; Combat Action Ribbon; PUC; MSM.

He has also written two articles that have been published in *Marine Corps Gazette*.

He is a trial attorney and lives in Seattle. He and his wife, Emily, have four daughters: Karen, Lynn, Lillian and Julia.

IRWIN H. GOLD, Captain, born Jan. 25, 1925 in Brooklyn, NY. Trained: 1943, Parris Island; 1944 Jacksonville Air Station, Camp Lejeune, Inf.

Units Served with: VMF (N)-542, ITEM Co, 3 Bn., 5th Marines, 1st MarDiv.

Memorable experiences include firefights in Korea. Capt. Gold left the service in 1956. He received the Purple Heart.

Education: BS degree from New York University.

Retired, he lives in Tucson, AZ with his wife, Joan. They have two daughters, Debra and Andrea.

ROBERT M. GOOCH, Lieutenant Colonel, born Nov. 20, 1919 in Troy, VA. Enlisted in the USMC in 1941 while still a student at the University of Virginia. Upon graduation in 1943 he as ordered to recruit training in Parris Island. From boot camp he was ordered to the officer candidate class at Quantico and was commissioned a 2nd Lt. in June 1943.

Following reserve officers class and Field Artillery School at Quantico he was ordered to the Pacific Theatre where he joined the 14th Defense Bn. as an air observer.

He participated in the liberation of Guam and while leading a patrol captured two Japanese prisoners. He next served in the Iwo Jima campaign as the assistant executive officer of a field artillery battery in the 12th Marines.

He was assigned to inactive duty in April 1945, but continued to serve as a reserve officer commanding reserve units in Baltimore, MD and Charlottesville, VA. Advancing through the ranks, he retired as a LtCol. in 1979.

He and his wife, Virginia, have two daughters, Pam and Pat, and two grandchildren.

WILLIAM H. "BILL" GOSSELL, Major General, born Jan. 26, 1932 in Libertyville, IL. Trained: NAVCAD,

Pensacola, 1954 Class 46/54; Wings June 1956.

Served with MAG-36, 1956-59; Active Reserves at NAS Glenview and NAS Dallas, 1959-91.

Memorable experiences and achievements include Operations at Desert Rock, NV, 1957, for last above ground Atomic Bomb test; and Operation Strongback, 1958, working with Philippine Army against HUKS on Luzon.

Maj. Gen Gossett retired in 1991. He received the Legion of Merit.

Currently, he is a consultant for aviation insurance. He and Marge have been married for 43 years and have two sons, Bob and Steve.

THOMAS J. GOUDREAU, Major, born June 4, 1962 in Bainbridge, MD. Trained at The Basic School, June 1984, Aviation Supply Corp School, April 1985

Served with HBMS-10, HBMS-13, MALS-13, UAV Joint Program Office, Headquarters Marine Corps.

Memorable experiences was being a member of core cadre of officers to standdown MCCRT6-10 and move/transition MAG-13 to Yuma, AZ.

His military awards include the Navy Achievement Medal, Joint Commendation Medal and Meritorious Service Medal.

He currently manages logistics services with UPS WWL. He and his wife, Debbi, have two sons, Michael and Matthew.

LARRY GRIFFIN, Captain, born June 19, 1947 in Louisville, KY. Following graduation from medical school, he was commissioned in the Medical Corps of the USNR. His entire naval service was spent in service with the Fleet Marine Corps.

Assignments include: Naval Hospital, Camp Lejeune, Amphibious Task Force Nine, 4th FSSG, 8th Tank Bn., 4th LAI Bn., USS *John F. Kennedy* (CV-67), USS *Inchon* (LPH-12), USS *Iwo Jima*.

A reserve officer, he was recalled to active duty with the 8th Tank Bn. USMCR, during Operation Desert Shield and served as battalion surgeon and CO of the medical detachment.

His military awards include the Navy and Marine Corps Commendation Medal, Combat Action Ribbon, National

Defense Service Medal, numerous campaign and commendation awards and medals and he was recommended for a Bronze Star (Desert Shield Operation).

He holds a BA with honors and MD from the University of Louisville and is board certified in Obstetrics and Gynecology. Currently, he is vice president of the American College of Obstetricians and Gynecologists.

He and his wife, the former Cara Anne Lee Ciliberti, have four children: Eric, Craig, Francesca, and Anthony, and two grandchildren, Michael and Parker.

GLENN L. HAAS, CWO4, born May 5, 1939 in San Francisco, CA. Trained: MCRD, San Diego, CA, 1962; NAS, Jacksonville, FL, 1962; NAS, Los Alamitos, CA, 1963; Camp Lejeune and MCAS Cherry Point, 1964; USAF Air University, 1967, US Army Special Warfare School, 1968, Camp Pendleton and MCAS, El Toro, NC, 1969-78; MCB, 20 Palms, 1981.

Served with MASS-4, MABS-47, H&MS-46, VMA-134, VMFA-134. Memorable experience was 32 years of camaraderie with fellow marines—nothing can top that.

Education includes BA and master's from the University of Redlands. Military Awards include National Defense Reserve Medal, Navy Commendations (5 awards). Currently he is a retired senior engineer with GTE of California.

Other significant achievements: five time recipient of the George Washington Honor Medal from the Freedoms Foundation at Valley Forge, PA; GTE Volunteer of the Year; Gatorade Coach of the Year and Little League Volunteer of the Year.

He and his wife, Lori, have one daughter, Pamela, and one son, Steven.

CHARLES D. HALE JR., CWO4, born June 16, 1931 in Appalachia, VA. Trained: Parris Island, 1949-50, Little Creek, Camp Lejeune, Coronado, CA, 1960-70.

Served with 1st Bn., 7th Marines (H&S), Korea, 4 ANGLICO, Royal Marines, 82nd Abn., Virginia National Guard, USNR (NAVCAD).

Memorable experiences were Hill 673, Korea, Mousetrap, Korea; merit promotion to GySgt. and receiving Purple Heart. He retired as CWO4 in February 1991 (broken time, 33 years, nine months, 28 days).

He is a retired fire investigator. He and his wife Jeanette have five children eight grandchildren.

TIMOTHY M. HANSON, Major, born Oct. 22 1960 in Springfield, MO. Enlisted in the USMC and went to boot camp at MCRD, San Diego, CA in June 1979, graduating in August 1979 with a meritorious promotion to private first class.

He served with the USMCR Engr. Maint. Co. in Omaha, NE while attending the University of Nebraska at Omaha.

After graduating in December 1986 he attended OCS in Quantico, VA, being commissioned a second lieutenant in April 1987. He attended The Basic School in Quantico, VA from April-October 1987, then assigned to the Artillery Officer Basic Course at Fort Sill, Lawton, OK, October 1987-March 1988.

In December 1990 he deployed to Saudi Arabia with 5/10 to serve as the intelligence officer and assistant operations officer during Operation Desert Shield and Desert Storm. He participated in the invasion of Kuwait and the liberation of Kuwait City.

The Marine Corps Mobilization Station, Chicago was his first reserve unit and he served with them from July 1994-June 1996. He served under Gen. (then Col.) Jack Bergman and then under Col. Scott Robertson. He was promoted to captain in December 1992 while in the Individual Ready Reserve.

He has served as OIC of the Peacetime/Wartime Support Team (PWST) in Omaha, NE, attached to the Engr. Maint. Co., Omaha from June 1996-September 1999. He was promoted to major in June 1998.

In civilian life he is employed as a police officer with the Papillion, NE Police Department and worked with the Palatine, IL, Police Department from 1992-97.

He is a graduate student in public administration at the University of Nebraska at Omaha and is planning on graduating with a master's degree in public administration in August 2001.

Married Robin R. Jessen in 1986 and they have one son, Gage.

RICHARD WAYNE HARDIN, Major, currently intelligence officer for 3rd Force Recon Co., Mobile and recruiting support officer, RS Montgomery. He was born Jan. 4, 1960 in Palestine, TX and attended Tyler public schools. A graduate of Tyler Jr. College and Southern Illinois University with a BS in aviation management.

Enlisted on his 23rd birthday and graduated from MCRD San Diego in August 1983. Graduating Air Traffic Control School at NAS, Memphis, he reported to SOM Sqdn., MCAS, El Toro, CA for tower ATC duty. Rising to the rank of sergeant, received his degree, assigned to OCS in June 1987 and commissioned in August.

Graduating TBS in February, 1988, he reported to Marine Air Control Sqdn.-7, Yuma, AZ. Graduating Air Defense Control Officers Course, 20 Palms, CA, he served as air intercept, CMS, intelligence officer, detachment commander for numerous deployments supporting Marine Aviation Weapons & Tactics Sqdn.-1, and a variety of joint and combined arms exercises in the US and Turkey. Participant in 1990 National Military Cycling Championship, Fort Carson, CO, placing 8th in category.

In December 1990 he was ordered to MACS-2 for Desert Storm as intercept officer, early warning radar site commander and CMS officer. Upon returning, he was released from active duty in June 1991.

Reserve units since December 1992: 2/14, Fort. Worth; Regimental Headquarters, 14th Marines, Dallas; MAG-41, Dallas; 4th ANGLICO, West Palm Beach, FL; HQ, 4/14, Bessemer, AL; Kilo Battery, 4/14, Huntsville, AL; graduate, Reserve Intelligence Officers Course, Norfolk, VA, 1995. Promoted to major, October 1997.

He is a defense systems trainer, technical writer and marketing/training materials designer for Brown International,

Huntsville, supporting several military exercises and operations including "Southern Watch" in Saudi, Bahrain and Kuwait as a civilian.

He is a member of MC Intelligence Association, National Military Intelligence Association, MCROA, MCL, American Legion and VFW.

He has two children, Laci J. Hardin and Cameron Stone.

HUGH W. HARDY, Major General, born Dec. 10, 1924 in Shattuck, OK. Enlisted in USMC Dec. 2, 1942 and commissioned through USMC Class 3D program Nov. 10, 1945. Graduated from Oklahoma University in 1947 then joined Humble Oil as a geophysicist.

Mobilized with B Co., 14th Inf. Bn., USMCR for Korean War, serving with 1st Replacement Draft, 1st Special Basic Class, and 1st Bn., 8th Marines including Mediterranean deployment before release to inactive duty. While employed with Humble Oil in Wichita Falls, TX and Houston, TX commanded 90th Spec. Inf. Co., H&S Co., 6th Inf. Bn., D Co., 4th AmTrac Bn., 1st Bn., 23rd Marines, 8th Staff Group and VTU 8-22.

Following promotion to colonel he served with and/or commanded RESMEBEX-70 (Operation High Desert); 56th, 81st and 85th MAUs during operations Pine Cone, DISEX-72 and Cutlass Sweep. After promotion to brigadier general served as Deputy CG, MCRD, San Diego, CA; ADC 4th Marine Division (Exercise Director RESMAULEX 2-75 HIDDEN WARRIOR and CG 5th MAB for RESMAULEX 1-76 LITTLE BROTHER.

Promoted to major general May 1, 1974 and served as deputy to CG, MCDEC, chairman of SecNav's Marine Corps Reserve Policy Board. Ordered to active duty June 25, 1980 to assume command of MCB, Camp Pendleton, CA. Retired Dec. 1, 1982.

In 1975 he was elected national president of MCROA and subsequently board chairman. He was later active in the ROA serving as Department of Texas

president and National Executive Committee Member (Marine Corps). He was the organizer of the first Marine Corps coordinating council in Houston, TX in 1963 and since then has worked with M&RA, HQMC and MarForRes in creating an additional 38 MCCCs across the US.

His education includes a BS in geological engineering from Oklahoma University, MS in industrial management from ICAF and an LHD from National University San Diego. He retired from Exxon Co., USA in March 1981 after 34 years of employment and joined Geoquest International, rising to become president before resigning in October 1986. Currently, he is president of Interpretation Consultants, Inc., an international petroleum exploration consulting company. He also is a member of the Executive Committee of the Sam Houston Area Council, Boy Scouts of America and vice chairman of the national Toys for Tots Foundation.

Major General Hardy wears the Legion of Merit

Medal, Navy Meritorious Unit Commendation Ribbon, Marine Corps Good Conduct Medal, Organized Marine Corps Reserve Medal w/4 Bronze Stars, American Defense Service Medal, Victory Medal (World War II), Navy Occupation Service Medal w/European Clasp, National Defense Service Medal, Military Outstanding Volunteer Service Medal, Armed Forces Reserve Medal and the Marine Corps Reserve Ribbon.

He and his late wife, the former Joyce Elaine Smith of Galveston, TX, have four daughters: Mrs. Karyn E. Parker of Alexandria, LA; Kathryn L. Hardy, Mrs. Karolyn L. Ratajczak and Mrs. Kay L. Lockard, all of Sugar Land, TX.

HAROLD FRANKLIN HARMAN, Lieutenant Colonel, born Feb. 21, 1914 in Elmore City, OK. Trained: Aug. 1, 1942-Jan. 1, 1943 Quantico, VA, January-

June 1943, Recruit Depot and Camp Pendleton.

Served with 1st Amph. Trac Bn., 1st MarDiv., December 1943-October 1945.

Memorable experiences and achievements include landing in first wave of troops Cape Arawe, Dec. 15, 1943; landed Cape Gloster, Dec. 26, 1943; landed Peleliu, Sept. 14, 1944; landed Okinawa, April 1, 1945.

Military Awards: Commanding General Commendation, Presidential Unit Citations (three awards), four Combat Stars Asiatic-Pacific Ribbon and others.

He retired after 40 years in the hardware business, 1946-86. He was married April, 4, 1942 to Helen Josephine Collins, who passed away April 20, 1989.

MASON D. "DOUG" HARRELL JR., completed OCS, TBS and the supply officer course 1968-69. From 1970-71 he served as assistant logistic officer, 4th Marines in Okinawa.

His reserve career began in 1972 at the 4th Recon. Bn., San Antonio, TX. In 1973 he became civil affairs officer in Washington, DC and served as an intelligence officer with CINCLANT staff from 1980-84. From 1984-89 he was OIC of the Reserve Attaché Program, spending three summers at the Tokyo Embassy as assistant naval attaché. During the Persian Gulf War he was the G-2 Rear for I MEF.

He was a seminar leader for the national security course each year 1991-98 and served as MARFORPAC process improvement officer 1996-98.

In his civilian career he is Chief US Administrative Law Judge in San Bernardino, CA where he presides over eight judges and their support staff.

He and his wife, Camille, have seven children.

ROGER KARR HARTER, Colonel, born Dec. 12, 1923 in Normal, IL. Trained: Parris Island, Quantico; radar, MIT; pre-radar, Harvard; Army radar, Camp Murphy, FL, Signal Bn., Camp Lejeune. Served with: 1st Marine Aircraft Wing HQ, MAG-128, MAG-24.

Memorable experiences and achievements include landing force commander, Operation High Grent, 52nd

MEU; chief of staff, Operation High Desert; CO, 13th Staff Group.

Current profession, professional registered parliamentarian. He is married to Claire Caverly Harter and they have four children.

JOHN J. HARVEY, Lieutenant Colonel, born May 29, 1955 in West Chester, PA. He was commissioned in August 1977. (BA political science, Lebanon Valley College, Annville, PA). Duty assignments have been: Basic School, May 1978; DNA, March 1980; 1980-84, UH-1N pilot, HML-267, HMLA-367 (2UDP), H&MS-39, MCAS, Camp Pendleton, CA; 1984-87, flight instructor, HT-8, NAS Whiting Field, Milton, FL (MA history, University of West Florida); 1987-90, HMLA-169 (HMM[C]-164 float) Camp Pendleton, CA; 1980-94, MAG-49 Detachment C, NAS South Weymouth, MA (HML-771/WestPac for DS/DS); 1994-96, MAG-46, Detachment A, Camp Pendleton, CA; 1996-98, action officer, PP&O, HQMC; August 1998, resident student, USMC War College.

Personal decorations include Meritorious Service Medal w/Gold Star, Air Medal, Navy/USMC Commendation Medal w/Gold Star and Navy/USMC Achievement Medal.

He is married to the former Bernice A. Ricciuti of West Chester, PA, and they have two daughters.

ROBERT H. HASHIMOTO, Captain, born July 3, 1958 in Chicago, IL. Trained: MCAS (M), New River, NC, 1977-79; MCAS (H), Futema, Okinawa, 1979-80; MCAS (M), New River, 1980-83; NAS, Genview, IL, 1983-95; Fort Sheridan, IL, 1995-98; NAS, JRB, Fort Worth, 1998-present.

Served with MATCS-28, MATCS-18, MATCS-48, H&MS-48, MTACS-48, MACS-24, ATC DET "A."

Memorable experiences and achievements include receiving direct commission from gunny sergeant to lieutenant (890919); being detachment commander, MACS-24 ATC Det. A.

Military awards include the MC Good Conduct (two), National Defense, Organized MC Resource Medal (four), Armed Forces Reserve Medal.

Currently, he is FAA air traffic controller.

GERALD R. HASLOP, Captain, born in Newark, OH. Trained: Parris Island, SC, OCS, Quantico, VA.

Served with: USS *Harris* (APA-2), flagship docked Tokyo Bay, Sept. 8, 1948, Yokohama, Japan.

Memorable experience was being on the first troop ship into Yokohama, Tokyo Bay, Sept. 8, 1945. The USS *Harris* APA-2 was the former President Grant, a South Pacific vessel.

He is a retired teacher from W&J College, Washington, PA.

PAUL F. HASTINGS, Major, born July 22, 1932 in Chambersburg, PA. Trained: Basic School, commissioned 1953. Enlisted USMCR 1950, called to active duty August 1950. Continued on active duty until retirement in 1972.

Served with: 1st MarDiv., 3rd MarDiv., Force Logistic Command, HQ, FMF Pacific, Marine Corps Air Station, Beaufort, SC.

Memorable experiences and achievements include being Marine Corps League National Commandant, 1979-81; representing governor of Pennsylvania at 50th anniversary of Pearl Harbor ceremony in Hawaii, Dec. 7, 1991; and being chairman, PA State Veterans' Commission.

His military awards include the Meritorious Service Medal; Navy Commendation Medal w/V; Pennsylvania Meritorious Service Medal. Inducted into Pennsylvania Veterans "Hall of Fame" in 1998.

He retired from USMC and is a retired chairman of the board, P. Hastings Corp.

He and his wife, Joan L. Lewis Hastings, have three children: Gary, Dona and Jodi.

WILLIAM A. "BILL" HAYWARD SR., Lieutenant Colonel, born Jan. 22, 1933 in Detroit, MI. He joined the USMC May 1, 1954, while attending college at Mississippi State University and received orders to report to active duty Nov. 1, 1954 at Quantico, VA for officer candidate training.

Commissioned February 19 and married on February 23, with the pretext to his bride that he could not make it in the Corps without her. He was part of 1-BC-55. Upon graduation from Basic School he was assigned to E Co., 2nd Bn., 4th Marines in Kaneohe Bay, Hawaii, at that time part of the First Provisional Air/Ground Brigade. He served in the Rifle Co. as machine gun commander, later as a rifle platoon commander, battalion legal officer, battalion adjutant and regimental personnel officer.

Discharged in December 1957, he came home to Gulfport, MS where he found the reserve unit to be equipped with land vehicle tracked howitzer sixes (LVTH-6). Having no mechanical ability or knowledge, the inspector instructor took him under his wing, Capt. Jerry Mathis, and he mastered the beast after spending his spare Sundays and nights studying the craft. He received an MOS as an 1803 and an artillery MOS. At that time, the reserve was made up entirely of volunteers, mostly veterans of WWII and Korea. His first "summer camp" was Camp Pendleton, CA, where they conducted direct fire on San Clemente Island and his respect for the troops increased immensely. His motivation for joining the reserve was to attain rank, as he certainly thought that we would be in another war and he had read the statistics on the survival rate of lieutenants.

In December 1964, he was appointed CO of "A" Co., 4th Amphibious Tractor Bn. This was during the Vietnam War and they thought they would be mobilized.

He attended his first MCROA conference in Boston in 1961 and was hooked on MCROA. Reuniting with friends he served with in Hawaii and drinking RUM punch at FANIEL HALL was great. He met his new inspector/instructor at the MCROA conference in Washington, DC and had a great time with young Capt. Bob Crabtree, a friend of Capt. Richard Buttolphs. The war was soon brought home to him as a month later, Bob Crabtree was in Gen. Hockmuth's helicopter when it was shot down in Vietnam. It was also at this conference that Gen. Leland Smith asked him to serve on the National Executive Council of MCROA. (At that time it was an "appointed" office). He told him he needed to check with his bank (he was employed by Gulf National Bank of Gulfport, MS at that time). He frankly didn't know how he would pay his way to the Executive Council meetings at that time in his civilian career. He related to his bank chairman the honor that had been bestowed upon him and the list of Marines who were serving on the Board at that time. He told him he would be happy to pay his way to these meetings and "hoped that a little of that talent would rub off on me." Hayward agreed.

They met in Gen. Arthur B. Hanson's office, and Col. Tom Wirt was the executive director of MCROA. He served for three years. The USMCR was continually redesignating and modernizing, and one of the things that they accomplished was to have new equipment sent to the Reserve Units on the same schedule as the Regulars. (This wasn't always done, but they lobbied for a token piece for training purposes until the appropriations caught up.)

He was extended for two years as company commander, and in 1968, started flying to Tampa, FL each month serving on the battalion staff. In 1970, he found a job in Tampa, FL and they moved. During this time his son, William A. (Chip) Hayward Jr., was enrolled in the Marine Military Academy in Harlingen, TX, which was established as a direct result of the support it received from MCROA and its members. He was appointed battalion commander of the 4th Assault Amphibian Bn. in 1974 and served three and a half years in that capacity. He devoted every weekend of his life during this tenure to the Corps as he had units in Norfolk, VA, Gulfport, MS, Jacksonville, FL, Galveston, TX and Tampa, FL. He retired in 1981 with 27 years service having attained the grade of lieutenant colonel.

He founded his own commercial mortgage brokerage firm in 1984, Hayward & Associates, a Florida corporation and they specialize in financing golf courses throughout the United State of America.

His wife, Joy, passed away Nov. 19, 1996.

DAVE HAZELL, Colonel, upon graduation from Boston University enlisted in the USMC in June 1968. In July 1969 began OCS at Quantico, VA,

graduating as the platoon honorman he was commissioned a 2nd lieutenant in March, 1969. After graduation from The Basic School he attended Communication Officers School (COS).

He served a tour in Vietnam from December 1969 to October 1970, and was assigned to the 26th Marines in Da Nang, the 9th Engr. Bn. in Chu Lai and the 7th Marines at LZ Baldy. He was released from active duty in December 1971 and returned to Boston University to complete his M.Ed.

He began his Marine Corps Reserve career in January 1972 with Marine Air Support Sqdn.-6 at NAS South Weymouth, MA. From 1972-83 he served as the communication officer and training officer, an air support control officer and eventually a senior air director. In 1983 he was selected for the Full Time Support Program and served on active duty at Headquarters Marine Corps as the programs monitor. While on active duty he set the three mile PFT record for Marines over 40 years of age. Upon completion of active duty he was assigned to the Mobilization Program. He was promoted to his present rank on Oct. 1, 1990 and retired on July 1, 1999. He received numerous awards and medals.

CHARLES S. "SID" HEAL, CWO5, born April 17, 1950 in Flint, MI. Trained: 1969, boot camp, MCRD, San Diego; 1976, Airborne School, Fort Benning, GA; 1980, MAGTF Staff Planning School.

Served with: Bravo Plt., 1st 8" Howitzer Battery SP, Vietnam; 3rd ANGLICO, Operation Desert Storm, Gulf War; 1 MEF, Operation United Shield, Somalia.

He has a BS degree in police science and administration from California State University at Los Angeles; MS in management, California Polytechnic University at Pomona; and master's in public administration, public administration, University of Southern California.

His awards include the Joint Service Commendation Medal, Navy/USMC Commendation Medal, Combat Action Ribbon (three awards).

He is currently a peace officer, Los Angeles Sheriff's Department.

He and his wife, the former Linda Diane Wagner, were married in 1970 and have five children: Kellee Michele, Kory Gene, Kasey Scott, Kassidy Robert, Kaydee Anne.

HUGH V. HINES, Major, born March 21, 1958 in Chapel Hill, NC. Trained in Jungle Warfare Training, Camp Sherman, Panama, 1998; Kernal Blitz, 1997; AOT, 1996; MORT Inspector, 1993-95; Regimental Firex, El Paso, 1992.

Served with OIC, PWST, Houston, TX, XO-1/23, Houston, TX, senior inspector, DET-6, Houston TX, 14th Marine Regt., H&S 2/14, "N" Battery 4/10, "H" Battery 3/10.

He feels that he spent most of his career with a radio handset stuck to his ear.

Military awards include Navy Commendation Medal, MUC, NUC, SMCR Medal, Armed Services Reserve, Marine Expedition Medal, Humanitarian Service Medal, National Defense Medal.

Current profession: president, Hines Insurance, Inc., sell/service group health insurance.

He and his wife, Jeanna, have two sons, Alexander and Christopher.

PETER H. "COACH" HOFINGA, Colonel, born July 24, 1933 in Brooklyn, NY. Trained September-December, 1956, 17th OCS Quantico, VA; January-December 1957, Flight Training NAS, Pensacola, FL; February-September 1958, Basic School 2-58, Quantico, VA; October 1958-December 1959, 2nd MT Bn., Camp Lejeune, NC.

Memorable experiences include USMCR January 1960-September 1987, 4th Force Recon., San Bernardino, CA, three years; 90 days active duty, 16 consecutive summers; MTU CA-11, six years; DET-119, Naval Special Warfare, Group One, Coronado, CA, three years.

He is retired from the University of California, Irvine, as a professor of physical education.

He is married with three children and nine grandchildren. One son is a Navy lieutenant commander F-14 pilot retired and now Delta captain; one son with Oracle Computer Co. in sales and management; one daughter is a Federal Express customer service associate.

J. DALE HOLLABAUGH, Colonel, entered the USMC immediately upon graduating with distinction with the Class of 1957, US Naval Academy, serving early in FMF infantry position such as platoon leader and AOps O of an afloat battalion in the Mediterranean. He earned his MSEE with distinction at NPS in 1963, followed by his assignment to HQMC to procure about $75M in FMF ground communications equipment.

His Vietnam tour included successive commands (as a captain and a major) of two 3rd MarDiv. FMF units in country. After resigning his regular commission as a major in 1967, he began concurrent careers in the Federal/Civil Service and the Marine Corps Reserve. Achieving command in every rank, qualified in nine specialties, he was ordered back to active duty in 1982 (Note 15 years after leaving active duty by Gen. P.X. Kelley, CMC) for 27 months to the staff of the Center for War Gaming, Naval War College, to lead the incorporation of the projection of power ashore into NWC's new computer support system. He completed his military career as OIC Mobilization Stations, Western States and Hawaii and retired as an 0-6 in 1987.

As an excepted civil servant, assistant professor Hollabaugh taught second class midshipmen in the electrical engineering department at the Naval Academy in 1967-68, then accepted an appointment to the Competitive Civil Service and achieved division, then deputy department (communications system)

head at the Naval Electronics Lab (formerly NEL, and NRaD) in San Diego, retiring as a GS-15 in 1978, thus beginning his civilian business career.

As a civilian, he has served in a series of responsible positions including vice president of the sixth largest executive search firm, operation manager of an engineering firm, international program manager for an aircraft equipment manufacturer, senior program manager for the National (digital electronic) Storage Industry Consortium (NSIC) in San Diego where he coordinated about $70M in pre-competitive research among the 35 company and 27 university members, and the government, and currently is a principal in his own technical consulting firm.

He reside in Ramona, CA (near San Diego) with his wife of 41 years, Nada. They have two children and eight grandchildren: son, Bret, lives with wife, Sheila, and daugher, Natalie in Elk Rapids, MI, and daughter, Linda, lives with husband, Brian Hill and children: Jennifer, Kelly, Lauren, Molly Jacob, Joseph and Hayley, in Clearfield, UT.

LEE B. HOLMES, Colonel, born Sept. 28, 1934 in Sioux City, IA. Trained: June 1956, Marca; 1957 4th BC, MCS, Quantico, VA.

Served with: 4th Marines, A&C Cos., 1st Bn., 1st Marine Brigade, 1957-59. Col. Holmes retired in November 1980.

He is married and has three children and four grandchildren.

WILLIAM R. HOLMES, Major, born in November 1922 in Granbury, TX. Commissioned from V-5 program, May 15, 1943. CalQual, USS *Wolverine*.

Served with VMSB-245. 936 and in combat with 142, MAG-32. Flew 51 missions, North Solomons, North Philippines and South Philippines.

Received DFC and Air Medal. Graduated Instrument Flight Instructors School, NAS, Atlanta. Instructed instrument training HQSQ, MAG-33 until release from active duty June 1946.

He also served as platoon leader, 11th Signal Co., Organized MCR, 1947-50. Recalled to active duty, assistant to director, 11th MCR District, 1951-53. Assigned to staff group, or-

ganized MCR, as military Govt-Civil Affairs officer and later as division adjutant, 1954-59. Retired June 1960. He was also elected first president of MCROA, Long Beach Chapter 1949-50.

He graduated from Long Beach State University, BA, economics, and taught in School of Business as assoc. prof., 1959-85. He also owned an insurance agency for 52 years.

He and his wife, Bonita, have two children and three grandchildren.

STEVEN T. HOLSTE, Captain, born March 9, 1953 in Port Townsend, WA. Trained: MCRD, San Diego, 1971; ITR, Camp Pendleton, 1971-72; Computer Sciences School, Quantico, VA, 1972; Officer Candidate School, Quantico, 1976; The Basic School, 1976-77; Computer Sciences School, Quantico, 1977; MCRD, Parris Island, SC, 1978.

Served with: Service Co., HQ Bn., MCSC, Barstow, CA, 1972-73; 4th Shore Party Bn., Seattle, WA, 1975-1976; HQ and Service Bn., 1st FSSG, Camp Pendleton, 1977-79; 4th Landing Support Bn., 4th FSSG, Seattle, 1980-81; Det "A", 3rd FSSG, MCAS, Iwakuni, Japan, 1981-82; 7th MAB, MCAGCC, 29 Palms, CA, 1982-84; Naval Postgraduate School, Monterey, CA, 1984-86; Computer Sciences School (staff), MCCDC, Quantico, 1986-89; 4th Tank Bn., 4th MarDiv., MCAS, Miramar, CA, 1997-present.

Memorable experiences and achievements include AFCEA honor graduate, Naval Postgraduate School (computer science), 1986.

Attended University of Washington and has BS in psychology, 1976; MBA in quantitative methods, 1981; PHD in Industrial/organizational psychology, 1995; Naval Postgraduate School, MS in computer science, 1986.

Military awards include MUC, NUC, SSDR, NDM.

Currently he is a research scientist at the Space and Naval Warfare (SPAWAR) Systems Center.

JAMES A. "JIM" HOMAN, Colonel, born Oct. 9, 1945 in Sioux City, IA. Training: Pensacola, 1968; TBS, 1967; Army War College, 1990-91.

VMA (AW)-225, 1969-70; MACG-48, 1975-85; USCINCPAC, 1989-91, MARFOREUR, 1996-97.

Memorable experience was RVN, 250 combat missions, AGA Intruder, 1969-70.

Col. Homan received 15 Air Medals and the JSCM. He retired in 1997.

Currently employed in aircraft parts sales. He and his wife of 32 years, June, have three children: Molly, Jimi, Brian, and five grandchildren.

EMILY HORNER, Lieutenant Colonel, born Feb. 25, 1917 in Moorestown, NJ. Trained: OCS, Camp Lejeune, Summer 1943; Communication School, Mt. Holyoke College, Fall 1943.

Served with: HQBN, MCAS, Mojave, CA, HQ, 4th MCRD, Philadelphia, PA, 1952-55.

Memorable experience was the time a fighter pilot landed his plane in Horner's communications office at MCAS Mojave, CA.

Now retired, Emily had two older sisters (one who served in the USNR), both are deceased.

RICHARD C. HYATT, Colonel, born Sept. 25, 1933 in Frederick, MD. Trained: Basic Class, March 1955; platoon leader, 2nd Tank Bn., Series Commander, MCRD.

Served with: San Diego, Co Cmdr. and S-3, 1st At Bn., CCO, USS *Princeton* (LPH-5, AWS, 1964-65, S-4, 2nd Tank Bn., Data Systems Div., HQMC; G-4, 2nd MarDiv. and III MAF, Comptroller, MCB, CLNC, Force Log. Cmd., Vietnam.

Memorable experiences and achievements include CCO, USS *Princeton*, CO, 25th Marines, 4th MarDiv., Marine Advisor Columbian Marine Corps.

Military awards include Navy Comm (two awards) one w/Combat V and Legion of Merit.

He is currently a musician and symphony orchestra manager and a slam and stand up poet.

He is married and has three sons and two daughters.

JACQUEES ANDRE ISTEL, Lieutenant Colonel, born in Paris, Jan. 28, 1929; came to US, 1940, naturalized, 1951; son of Andre and Yvonne Mathilde Cremieux I.; married Felicia Juliana Lee,

June 14, 1973, and has one daughter by a previous marriage, Claudia Yvonne has AB degree from Princeton, 1940. Stock analyst, Andre Istel & Co., NYC, 1950-55; pres. Parachutes Inc., Orange, MA, 1957-87, Intramgmt. Inc., NYC, 1962-80; chmn. Pilot Knob Corp., 1982–; mayor, town of Felicity, CA, 1986–; curator ctrl. Point for Memories, CA, 1992–; pres. VI World Parachuting Championships, 1962; capt., US Parachuting team, 1956, capt., team leader, 1958; chmn. MA Parachuting Commn., 1961-62; lifetime hon. pres. Internat. Parachuting Commn., Fedn. Aero. Internat., 1965–; chmn. Hall of Fame of Parachuting, 1973–; founder Nat. Collegiate Parachuting League, 1957. Author: *Coe the Good Dragon at the Center of the World,* 1985, *Coe le Bon Dragon au Centre du Monde,* 1985. Contbr. articles to encys., profl. publs. Trustee Inst. for Man and Sci., 1975-82; bd. dirs. Marine Corps Scholarship Found., 1975-85. Served with USMC, 1952-54; lt. col., Res. Recipient Leo Stevens Award, 1958, Diplome Paul Tissandier, 1969. Mem. Nat. Aero. Assn. (bd. dirs. 1965-68), Fedn. Internat. des Centres (pres. 1990–), Cercle de l'Union Interallé (Paris), Marine Corps Res. Officers Assn., DAV (life), Racquet and Tennis Club (NYC), Princeton Club (NYC). Holder world record, parachuting, 1961; patentee in field; co-leader Nat. Geog. Soc. Vilcabamba Expdn., 1964; Imperial County Groundwater Commission, 1997–. Home: Northview, Felicity, CA also: 10 rue Galilée, Paris, France, Office: 1 Center of the World Plz, Felicity, CA.

BARRY W. JACKSON, Major, born Jan. 27, 1930 in Long Branch, NJ. NROTC Stanford, commissioned 1952. 4th Marines EmbO; then platoon leader and XO, E Co., Pendleton. Nara, Japan, regimental. MP officer, patrolling Nara. Award from Nara Rotary for donating four one-year college scholarships. Early feminist, so suspected of being communist, cleared after resigning regular commission. 7th Marines,

Korea, then 2nd ITR tactics instructor, ran "three day war".

At Stanford Law School, served in reserve AA Battery, sent to Alaska to explore establishing reserve VTUs. Settled in territory, 1958, established VTUs in Fairbanks, Anchorage, Sitka. later CO, Composite Co. 17-3, USNR.

Alaska House of Representatives, finance com., 1965-66; chair judiciary, 1969-70, despite being in minority. Principal drafter, architect, Alaska Native Claims Settlement Act. Chaired democratic state conventions, 1974, 1976, 1978, 1990; 1996 Legislature Citation for contributions to Alaska. Continues solo practice in Fairbanks. Divorced, five children and 13 grandchildren.

GARY L. "JACK" JACKSON, Major, born Nov. 16, 1954. Trained: 1974, OCS, Quantico, VA; 1977, Artillery School, Fort Sill, OK; 1987, AWS; 1992, CGSC, Quantico, VA.

Served with: 1st Battery, 3rd Bn., 10th Marines, 2nd MarDiv.; BLT 1/8; 4th Bn., 10th Marines, 2nd MarDiv.; HQ, 6th Marine Corps District; 4th Tank Bn., 4th MarDiv.; K, L&M Battery, 4th Bn., 4th MarDiv.; HQ, 2nd MEB, HQ Bn., Quantico.

Memorable experiences and achievements include 1978-80, fire support coordinator, BLT 1/8; 1980, Cuban Boat Lift; 1981-82 battery commander; 1982-84, operations officer, 6th Marine Corps District.

Military awards incluce Meritorious Service Medal; Navy Commendation Medal w/2nd Award; Navy Achievement Medal.

Current profession: US Department of Defense, special agent.

Other significant achievements: 1994-95, commander of American Legion Post 59, Dunn, NC; 1996-97, commander of American Legion 13th District of the Department of NC.

He has two daughters: Elizabeth Ann (20) and Jennifer Elaine (15).

RAYMOND F. "RAY" JACOBSEN, Captain, born July. 12, 1944 in Estherville, IA. Trained: 1963, 1965-66,

Quantico, VA, 1966-67, Camp Lejeune, NC.

Served with 3rd 155mm Gun Btry. (SP); 11th Marines, RVN, April 1967-May 1968; Admin. Services, Albany, GA, June 1968-June 1969; 26th Rifle Co., Twin Cities, MN, June 1969-May 1971.

Military awards include the National Defense, Vietnam Service, Combat Action Ribbon, Presidential Unit Citation.

He is retired and has never been married.

FARNHAM J. "GUNNER" JOHNSON, 1st Lieutenant, born June 23, 1924. Trained: Marine V-12, MI, 1943-44; Parris Island, 1944; Lejeune, 1944; Quantico, 1945; Pendleton, 1945.

Served with FMF PAC, Forward Echelon, Island Command, Guam.

Memorable experiences and achievements include being NFL player, 1947-48; International BF Goodrich Co., 1950-88, Akron, OH, Washington, DC; Hawaii, Netherlands, Sweden, Denmark, Philippines, New York City.

Earned BS in economics from University of Wisconsin, 1948; BFT from American Institute for Foreign Trade, 1950; Thunderbird, American Graduate School of International Management, 1978.

He is a widower. Currently, he is an international consultant.

HARRY A. JOHNSON JR., Colonel, born May. 15, 1921 in Batesville, MS. Trained: 1941, Parris, Island; 1942, OCC, ROC Quantico, VA; 1943, Tutuila, American Samoa; 1945, Quantico; 1945, Fort Sill, OK.

Served with: Rifle Rn. Det., Parris Island; 2nd Def. Bn., 5th Amph. Corps Arty., Tarawa, Leyte, Philippines; 1st Service Bn., 5th Motor Transport Bn., VTU6-17, Intelligence (Russian language).

Memorable experiences and achievements include surviving training at Parris Island, Quantico and Infantry School, American Samoa, Tarawa, Leyte, Philippine Islands and being able to get up and move every morning.

Military awards include Presidential Unit Citation, Good Conduct Medal, Organized Marine Corps Reserve Medal, American Defense Service Medal, American Theatre, Asiatic-Pacific w/2 stars, WWII Victory Medal, National Defense Service Medal, Armed Forces Reserve, MC Res., Philippine Liberation (two stars), Philippine Independence, Philippine Pres. Unit Citation.

Currently he is owner of Commercial and Military Computers, Inc.

He and his wife of 53 years, Penny, have two children, Harry III and Janet, and five grandchildren.

JERRY K. "GAUCHO" JOHNSON, Colonel, born June 22, 1945 in Williston, ND. Trained: OCS, Quantico, VA, 1970; USA Flight School, Fort Wolters, TX, Fort Rucker, AL.

Served with HMA-269, HMA-369, HMA-169 (Active Duty); HMA-773, HMM-764, HMH-777, HMH-769 (Reserve Duty).

Memorable experiences and achievements include being "Plankholder", all three ACDU Cobra Squadrons, nominated, Helo Pilot of the Year, 1973; CO, HMH-769, 1991-94.

His awards include Meritorious Service Medal, Air Medal (10), CAR, NDM (two), numerous unit and campaign ribbons.

Currently he is the owner of Genesis Packaging Co.

He and his wife, Julie, have two daughters, Jenni and Jessica.

ROBERT M. JOHNSTONE, Lieutenant Colonel, born April 20, 1944 in Bellingham, WA. Combat commands included platoon commander, 3rd Plt., C

Co., 1st Tank Bn., 1st MarDiv. (Rein) FMF, and company commander, Co. B, 5th Tank Bn., RLT-27, 5th MarDiv., 1st MarDiv. (Rein) FMF during combat operations in the Republic of Vietnam, 1967-68. As a 1st lieutenant, he participated in numerous operations against insurgent communist Viet Cong forces in the RVN, including Operation Ballistic Charger, Operation Allenbrook and Operation Hue City during the Tet Offensive of 1968. The battle for Hue City during the 1968 Tet Offensive was the most memorable combat experience of his career.

Upon discharge from active duty in 1969, he continued to participate in the organized Marine Corps Reserve and served as CO of Service Co. 6th Engr. Bn., 4th MarDiv. FMF, Salem, OR. He retired in 1986 with the rank of lieutenant colonel and has been a practicing lawyer since 1972. His firm is Robert M. Johnstone, P.C., in McMinnville, OR. He is a lecturer and has authored *Doing Business in Russia,* PSI Publications, 1995 (2nd edition, 1996). He has traveled extensively in Russia and the former Soviet Union. Connected with this work, Bob has received the following awards: the prestigious "Award for Distinguished Citizen Contribution to Russian-American Business" from *Delovie Lyudi/Business in Russia Magazine,* presented to him at the Russian Embassy in 1995, the People to People "Torch of Birmingham Award" for his work in promotion Russian-American relations and, additionally, a Commendation from the President of the United States in 1996 "In recognition of outstanding contributions to the economic growth and development of Russia and CIS during their historic transition." He was a delegate to the US/China joint session on trade, investment and economic law, held in Beijing, Peoples Republic of China, at the Great Hall of the People, in 1987. He was also a delegate to the Moscow Conference on law and economic cooperation, held at the Kremlin, in Moscow, Russia in 1990, and a sponsor of The Moscow Business Conference, also held at the Kremlin in 1991. Additional published works include: *Ethics: Review of Malpractice Cases in Estate Planning,* published by Oregon Law Institute, 1990; *Intellectual Property,* Pepperdine University Russian

Conversion Program, US Committee to Assist Russian Reform, 1996; *How to Handle School Employee Misconduct,* published by Lorman Educational Service, 1997; *School Liability for Computer/Internet Access,* published by Professional Development Network, 1997; *Areas of School Liability Relating to Internet Access,* published by Lorman Education Service, 1998.

He is also an owner of Lost Horse Creek Lodge, Hamilton, MN, a year-round destination resort and gateway to beautiful Montana. He is also a principal in Seabridge Capital, LLC, a venture capital firm.

He is married to Julianne and has six children. Of his Marine Corps career, he is most proud to have served under the legendary and preeminent tank leader LtCol. Eugene "Gene" Berbaum, and Col. C.W. "Chuck" Wilson. During his military career, he acquired three MOS's 1802, 1302 and 4402.

GEORGE A. JONIC JR., Colonel, born April 13, 1942 in Sommerville, NJ. Commissioned through the PLC program in 1964, he served with the 2nd MarDiv. in Guantanamo Bay, Cuba before reporting to the 3rd MarDiv., Dong Ha, Vietnam in 1967. As company commander in 9th Motor Transport Bn., he ran frequent "Rough Rider" convoys throughout Northern I Corps. He was awarded the Navy Commendation Medal w/Combat V, the Vietnamese Cross of Gallantry, Presidential Unit Citation and other campaign and commendation medals.

Returning to CONUS in 1968, he served as aide-de camp to the commanding general, 3rd Mar Aircraft Wing, MCAS, El Toro, CA and continued as aide to Maj. Gen. Arthur H. Adams, USMC in his 6 month assignment as senior member, Military Armistice Commission, United Nations Command, Seoul, Korea.

In 1970 he was released from active duty but continued in the Reserves with a variety of command and staff assignments in the 6th Motor Transport Bn. at Fort Monmouth, NJ and the 6th Comm. and was battalion commander of 6th Motor Transport Bn., 4th FSSG from 1982-84. He attended numerous landing force planning courses at Coronado and Command and Staff College at Quantico. His last assignment prior to retiring in 1990 was OIC, Marine Corps Mobilization Station, New Haven, CT.

His education includes a BA in english from Iona College in New Rochelle, NY and a year at Fordham Law School in New York City. Since 1970 he has been in numerous sales and marketing management positions with the IBM Corp. and is currently with IBM Global Services in Somers, NY. He and his wife, Carol, and their three children, Andy, Greg and Kathleen, live in Ridgefield CT and Chatham, MA.

JOHN P. JOYCE, Captain, born in Chicago IL. Trained and served with: "G" TBS, Quantico, 1975; M 3/8 NAS, Camp Lejeune, 1976-77; H&S 2/6 Lejeune, 1978; MACG-48, Glenview, 1978-90.

Memorable experiences and achievements include winning 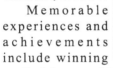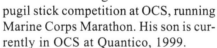 pugil stick competition at OCS, running Marine Corps Marathon. His son is currently in OCS at Quantico, 1999.

Currently, he is a lieutenant with the Chicago Fire Department.

JOHN M. KAHENY, Colonel, born in the Bronx, Nov. 28, 1944. He joined the PLC program in 1962, at Mt. St. Mary's College, Emmitsburg, MD and was commissioned in 1966.

He joined the 1st Bn., 26th Marines in Vietnam, serving as a rifle platoon and company commander. Upon his release from active duty in 1970, he enrolled at Hastings College of the Law, and joined the 3rd Bn., 23rd Marines.

In 1973 he began a 23 year career with the San Diego City Attorney. After tours with the 4th Tank Bn. and the 16th Staff Group, he joined the 2nd Marine Amphibious Brigade, before returning to the 4th Tank Bn. as battalion commander in 1985. During Operation Desert Storm, he commanded the 3rd Civil Affairs Group (Rein). He retired in 1995.

In 1990, he was elected as the national president of the Marine Corps Reserve Officers Assn. In 1996, he became the city attorney of Chula Vista, CA.

His personal decorations include the Bronze Star Medal w/Combat V and the Meritorious Service Medal.

ALPHONSE A. KANUSAS, Lieutenant Colonel, born Dec. 21, 1920 in Chicago IL. WWII Training at Memphis, Pensacola, Jacksonville, El Toro, NAS. Korea Training at Quantico VA, choppers.

Served with VMF-231 and 442, flying the Corsair F4U in Marshal Islands and Okinawa, 2nd tour in Korea, VMO-6, Helicopters, Reserves, Cougars F9F.

Memorable experiences and achievements include flying Corsairs and he didn't have an automobile driver's license. Received his first automobile license while in Marshall Islands.

Military awards include Distinguished Flying Cross, two Air Medals, two Presidential Unit Citations, Army and Marine Reserve Medals, American Theatre, Asiatic-Pacific Campaign Medal, Victory Medal, China Sea, Korean Theatre and United Nations.

Currently he is the owner/manager of Productive Equipment Corp.

He has three children and seven grandchildren and his parents where Lithuanian immigrants.

SYLVAN J. KAPLAN, in addition to being a co-founder of Kaplan Associates, has a primary specialty as a clinical and consulting psychologist.

His career, however, has been broad in scope and extensive in depth, and has not been restricted to

his primary specialty. He has conducted research in radiobiology, performed systems analyses in biomedical and educational fields, engaged in long range planning and futures research at the White House and federal departmental levels. He has held executive administrative positions in academia and in federal government. His experiences include cross national activities in personnel selection for the US Peace Corps. As a multi-faceted theoretician and pragmatist, he has worked on problems in computer technology, engineering, military science, urban and rural development, population, and human ecology. He is the author or co-author of more than 60 scientific publications.

His professional affiliations include membership in many national associations. He has been president of the Texas Psychological Association and of the Mid-Atlantic Division of the American Association for Marriage and Family Therapists. He holds a Diplomate in clinical psychology granted him by the American Board of Professional Psychology.

He is a retired colonel in the USMCR, and remains active in his interest in military and geopolitical affairs. He is listed in *Who's Who In American Men and Women Of Science*.

WILLIAM O. KARCHER, Lieutenant Colonel, born July 9, 1919 in Lee County, TX. Philadelphia Navy Yard, March 1942-July 1942. Ordered to Camp Elliott, CA with the 6th Marine Regt., July 1942 and went to Guadalcanal, then Tarawa and Saipan.

Reassigned in 1944 after Saipan and attended quartermaster school at Camp Elliott and assigned to USS *Cambria* (APA-36) in May 1945 as transport quartermaster. Was privileged to observe the peace signing at Nagasaki, Japan.

He received the Purple Heart.

Karcher is now retired and enjoying life with his wife of 58 years.

FRANCIS J. "FRANK" KAVENEY, Captain, born Oct. 11, 1943. Trained: Quantico, VA; Platoon Leaders Class, 1964; The Basic School, September 1967-March 1968; Naval Justice School, March-May 1968.

Served with Division Legal, HQ Bn., 1st MarDiv., June 1968-July 1969,

Da Nang, Rep. of Vietnam; Naval Appellate Review Activity (Government Counsel), August 1969-August 1971.

Memorable experiences and achievements include serving as platoon commander and company commander of 1st MarDiv. Reaction Force including Tet Offensive of February 1969; served as defense counsel on murder case at Da Nang, resulting in acquittal.

Military awards include Two Navy Commendation Medals w/Combat V, Combat Action Ribbon, and misc. campaign ribbons.

Currently he is an attorney. He and his wife, Cathy, have two sons and two daughters: Kevin (graduated West Point in 1996), Brian (2nd Lt., USMC), Maura (19) and Colleen (10).

PRESTON P. "PP" KELLOGG, Colonel, born May 30, 1930 in New York, NY. Trained July 1950-February 1952, NAS, Pensacola, FL.

Served with: VMF-533, MCAS, Cherry Point, NC; VMA-121, K-3, Korea; VMA-251, Japan, VMF-244, NAS, Columbus; VMF-351, 4MAW, Atlanta, GA.

Memorable experiences and achievements include receiving MS degree in industrial management, at Georgia Institute of Technology, M/A chief pilot, 1977-82, Republic Airlines.

His awards include the Air Medal, Marine Corps Reserve, National Defense Medal, US Korean Service; UN Korean Service.

He is a Retired NWA Airline pilot. He and two sisters grew up in Willoughby, OH.

JOSEPH KERKE, Lieutenant Colonel, born July 21, 1949 in Chicago, IL. Commissioned upon completion of 80th OCC, OCS, 1972, attended E Co. 5-73 TBS and FAOBC 501-74.

Active duty: 1972-75, B-1/10 at GTMO 1977, BLT 2/8, 32nd MAU; RAU CLNC; 1978, MECEP Prep School, chemistry instructor; 1979-84, K-4/14, CO 1982-84, Joliet, IL; 1985, HQ and Svc. Co. 2/24, FSO.

Completed MCAWSEC, 1978; MCC and SCEC, 1986; FAOAEC, 1987; IOAEC, 1988; AFSCROC, 1987.

Awarded Navy Commendation Medal in 1984.

Attended Morton Junior College, AS, 1969; Illinois State University, BSEd., 1972; DePaul University, MS w/Distinction, 1987.

He was a high school chemistry teacher in the Chicago Public Schools, 1975-1933 and at Hillcrest High School, Country Club Hills, IL, since 1993.

Son of Joseph T. Kerke (deceased), GM 3/c, USN (WWII) and Mary Chillman Kerke, CPL, USMCWR (WWII).

He is married to the former Hattie L. Smith.

ROBERT J. "BOB" KIMARTIN, Major, born Jan. 17, 1959 in Lowell, MA. Trained: Parris Island, 1976, OCS, Quantico, 1977 and 1979.

Served with: MCAS (H), New River, NC, 1984-87; MCB, Camp Pendleton, CA, OSJA, 1996-present; many reserve units.

Currently he is an attorney and judge advocate. He is married and two children.

GARY J. KNISS, Lieutenant Colonel, born Dec. 5, 1944 in Portland, OR. Enlisted July 16, 1961, commissioned Sept. 1, 1969, retired Sept. 1, 1998 after 37 years of service.

Trained: MCRD, San Diego, Quantico, VA, Camp Pendleton, Camp Lejeune, Camp Butler, Camp Elmore.

Served with: 1st, 2nd, 3rd, 4th and 5th Divs.

He retired as a Captain of the Tualatin Valley Fire & Rescue, Beaverton, OR in 1998.

He and his wife have one daughter (20) who attends Brown University and one son (12) who is in middle school.

WILLIAM J. "BILL" KOEHLE, Lieutenant Colonel, born Nov. 29, 1950 in Kankakee, IL. Trained: 1972, Quantico, VA; 1973, Camp Lejeune; 1991, Camp Pendleton.

Served with: 8th Engr. Bn., 34th MAU, Truck Co., 4th MarDiv., 3/25, 4th MarDiv.

Memorable experiences and achievements include being recalled to active duty for Desert Storm.

His awards include the National Defense Service Medal w/star and "M", Armed Force Reserve Medal w/Hourglass, OMCR Medal w/4 stars, Meritorious Unit Commendation.

Currently he is a manufacturing consultant. He is married and has three children and one grandson.

TED KOLANKIEWICZ, Colonel, soloed at the ripe old age of 16. He graduated from high school in June 1943 and began active duty as a cadet in the V-5 program in September 1843, 17 years old. He was commissioned a 2nd lieutenant 31 months later and believes this is the record for continuous duty as a cadet. He remained on active duty flying F4Us, occasionally from CVEs, until September 1947.

He was recalled to active duty with VMF-451 from NAS Willow Grove in March 1951, requalified on the Valley Forge and went to Korea in October. He flew 101 missions with VMFs-312 and 323, and earned the DFC and 5 Air Medals. Following his combat tour, he set up, furnished and managed the Officer's Club at K-6. After discharge, Lt. Kolankiewicz remained active with the Organized Reserve until 1976. Col. Kolankiewicz's last assignments were CO of the Marine Air Reserve Group at NAF Andrews, then the Staff Group at NAS Memphis.

His 30-odd years of experience include apprentice mechanic, railroad brakeman, crop duster, and reciprocating and jet engine test engineer. With the FAA, he has been a maintenance chief, engineering and certification test pilot, all-weather research pilot, and program manager on a variety of R&D efforts including the SST and V/STOL Programs.

Between and after the wars, he earned a BS in ME, and, while with the FAA, was awarded a fellowship to obtain a MS in CE (transportation). He is a member of the Society of Experimental Test Pilots (SETP), MENSA, MCROA, MCAA, TROA, American Legion, and the VFW. He has flown about a hundred models of airplanes ranging from the size and weight of the J3 Cub to the speed of the F8 and size of the Convair 880 and Boeing 707.

He and his wife, Pauline, reared four sons and are retired, living in the house they built themselves on the bayfront in Brigantine, NJ. They enjoy fishing, sailing, tennis, reunions, partying, computers and surfing the internet.

BEVERLY B. KRAMMES, Colonel, born April 17, 1914 in Newark, OH. He joined the Marines as an Aviation Cadet in 1937. He was a fighter pilot with many missions to his credit.

He was a member of the "Black Sheep Sqdn." led by the legendary "Pappy Boyington", and flew missions near Australia to keep the Japanese out of the islands. Included in his military memorabilia were photos of the entire Black Sheep Sqdn, One of the group photos was circulated throughout the US and autographed by the crew 35 years after the photo was taken.

As a member of this group, Krammes flew into combat zones and flew wounded Marines out of danger and to hospitals in Sidney, Australia. For his courageous efforts he was awarded the Distinguished Flying Cross, three Air Medals and other campaign and commendation medals. The original naval citations for bravery, along with the photos and other military memorabilia, are now displayed in the Military Air Preservation (MAPS) MAPS Air Museum, Akron-Canton Regional Airport, North Canton, OH.

He continued his association with the Marine Corps, affiliating with The Retired Officers Association (TROA), the Reserve Officers Association (ROA), the Association of Naval Aviation (ANA).

He graduated from Heidelberg College and the University of Michigan with an engineering degree. Krammes left the military in 1947 and returned to North Canton. He worked for the Hoover Co. for 33 years and retired as an executive engineer in 1979.

LARRY E. LAWLER, Colonel, born July 28, 1931 in Akron, CO. He enlisted in the Marine Corps after high school and one year of college in Scottsbluff, NE in August, 1951. After boot camp at San Diego, he served as legal clerk for the 7th Engr. Bn. at Camp Pendleton. Corporal Lawler was selected for a screening course at Quantico and was commissioned in November 1952.

In Korea, he served with the 7th Motor Transport Bn. as platoon and company cmdr. He was then assigned as motor transport officer for the 1st MarRegt., 1st MarDiv. until his release from active duty in November 1954.

He obtained his BA from Northern Colorado University and then earned his law degree from the University of Colorado at Boulder in 1960. He maintained his affiliation with the Marine Corps in the active reserves at Buckley Field near Denver, CO in Marine Air Control Sqdn. 23. Thereafter, he was instrumental in founding a JAG volunteer training unit at the Denver Federal Center and served as its CO. Col. Lawler served on the national board of directors of MCROA in 1976.

He is married to Peggy Lawler and between them they have seven children (one deceased), 17 grandchildren and two great grandchildren. He has practiced law in the west suburbs of Denver since 1960. He is a life member of MCROA and the 1st MarDiv. Association, and is a member of the Marine's Memorial Club in San Francisco, the Marine Corps League and various other organizations.

CHARLES A. LAZZARO, Lieutenant Colonel, born April 10, 1931 in San Diego, CA. Married to Patricia and has two sons, Gary Lee and Terry Scott. Received AB and MA from San Diego State College, 1953. He did graduate work in school administration at California Western University, University of Hawaii, SDSC and UCLA.

Service highlights: Attended 9th OCC and commissioned, December 1953, 1st BC, 1954 at Quantico, VA. Reported to flight training at NABTC, Pensacola, 1954 and NAATC, Corpus Christi/Kingsville ATU 107-8, 1955.

He was assigned to VMA-212, MAG-13, Devil Cats of the 1st Marine Brigade, MCAS, Kaneohe Bay, Oahu, flying AD Skyraiders in Operations MAUKA and TRADEWINDS, 1955-57. Deployed on TAD to Japan/Philippines for Operation Beacon Hill. Released from active duty, 1957.

Continued in Class III in VTU-12-70, 1961-64. Joined OMCR Class II with 3rd ANGLICO, 1964-72, at NS Long Beach as FAC/ALO, S-3, XO and Detachment CO. Participated in ATDs in Operations Wildcard and Sidewinder, 1966, Golden Slipper, 1967, Bell Banger, 1968, Pike Pole and Beat Tempo, 1969 and High Desert, 1970, supporting reserve and regular infantry battalions at MCB-29BN., LMS, NAAS Fallon/NAD Hawthorne, MCB Camp Pendleton and NAS Whidbey Island. Returned to Class III with MTU-CA 6, 1972-79. Retired in 1979 after 26 years.

Military schools: Escape and Evasion, Dillingham AFB; Special Weapons External Delivery, MCAS El Toro; Junior Courses 1-2, MCB, Camp Pendleton; Landing Force Staff Planning 1-2-3-12, TACP Course, Aviation Staff Planning, Naval Gunfire Staff Planning, NAB, Coronado; Command and Staff 1-2, MCB, Quantico; Industrial War College,

NSS, NTC, San Diego; and National Defense University, NSS, Fort Bragg.

Civilian Occupation: Teacher, audio-visual consultant, vice-principal ad principal, 31 years.

JOHN WARREN "JACK" LEAPER, Colonel, born May 5, 1922 in Minneapolis, MN. Trained: 1942, Iowa preflight, 1942, MPLSE Base; 1943, Pensacola; 1943 Opalocka; 1943, El Toro, Fighter Training.

Served with VMF-314, VMF-234, Cherry Point, VMF-543

Memorable experiences and achievements include being a life member of Society of Experimental Test Pilots.

Military awards include the Navy Cross, Purple Heart and Air Medal.

He graduated Marine Air Infantry School, 9th Class, April 1946; Marine Corps Commandant and Staff College, July 1960; received Juris Doctorate, Fernando College of Law, January 1975.

He is a retired consultant.

He and his wife celebrated 50th wedding anniversary Nov. 19, 1995. They have nine children and 12 grandchildren.

RICHARD JAY "DICK" LEASE, 1st Lieutenant, born Dec. 10, 1914 in Cherokee, OH. Began his military reserve army training at the University of Arizona in 1933.

On Dec. 7, 1941 he was at the Pima Pistol Club west of Tucson when a radio began to tell of the Pearl Harbor attack. Expecting to be called soon to active duty, he immediately gathered up his gear and made preparations. The weeks wore on and finally he learned that there were no plans to call him on AD because he was a patrol sergeant in a police department. It

was then that he decided to enlist in the Marine Corps.

Enlisted shortly after the birth of his son and trained December 1942-July 1943, Quantico, VA. Served with 1st MarDiv. Ord., rifle troop platoon leader with the 2nd Bn. as a result of his performance in battle during the Pelelieu Campaign, 5th Regt.

Discharged as 1st lieutenant in November 1946. He is currently retired and living in Las Cruces, NM.

JAMES L. LEWIS, Major, born Nov. 10, 1936 in Shreveport, LA. Commissioned through the PLC Program, he completed flight school in Pensacola in 1958. He served in the Far East with HMR (L) 261 in 1959-60, joining HMR (L) 262 at MCAF New River where he was the prime recovery pilot for Gus Grisson's Mercury-Redstone 4 mission.

He joined the National Aeronautics and Space Administration in 1962 and served in various astronaut engineering support and NASA management areas until his retirement in January 2000.

In the late 60s and early 70s, he successfully raced formula cars in the SCCA, applying the winning touch at various tracks in the US and Mexico.

His education includes Bachelors, 1957, Masters, 1962; and Ph.D, 1979, degrees from the University of Houston.

He married his wife, Ghislaine, in 1973. They have two sons, Chris and Phil, who graduated from the University of Texas as chemical engineers in 1997 and 1999.

He retired from the USMCR in 1983 and is a life member of MCROA and VFW.

GERARD GEORGE LIEBENGUTH, 1st Lieutenant, born Feb. 21, 1921 in New York, NY. Training: Parris Island; Quantico, 1942; Naval Advanced Electronic Training Schools, Dearborn, MI and Washington, DC, 1945.

Served with 10th Defense Bn., 1st MAC, Solomon Islands and 10th Defense Bn., 5th MAC, Marshall Islands, June 1942-July 1944.

Memorable experiences and achievements include combat actions, Florida and Russell Islands, Solomons, Enewetok, Marshals.

Education: BS, commerce, University of North Carolina; Graduate study, business administration, Oklahoma University.

His military awards include Navy/Marine Unit Commendation, American and Asiatic-Pacific campaigns and WWII Victory.

He is retired from the Chevron Corporation. He is married and has four children and seven grandchildren.

JOHN J. "JACK" LISTER, Lieutenant Colonel, born Sept. 2, 1927 in Philadelphia, PA. Trained: Summer 1945, Parris Island, SC; Summer 1951, Quantico, VA.

Served with: 1st MarDiv., 1945-46 in North China (Peking); B Co., 7th Marines, 1st MarDiv., 1952-53, Korea.

China service as a private was a memorable experience. They disarmed and repatriated the Japanese. The outpost duty as a platoon leader in Korea was also not to be forgotten. The courage of the Marines was in the finest traditions of the Corps.

Military awards received are Bronze Star w/Combat V, China Service Medal, Korean Service Medal w/2 stars, Presidential Unit Citation w/2 stars.

Education: St. Joseph's College, 1951; Villanova University School of Law, 1956.

Currently, he is a pension consultant. He is married and has six children, three step children and 23 grandchildren.

RODNEY S. "ROD" LOOSE, Major, born Nov. 6, 1948 in West Reading, PA. Training: Quantico, MCB-PLC (OCS), 1968-69; Basic School, September 1970-March 1971; Amph. Warfare School, 1983; Command and Staff (correspondence), 1996; Hawk Missile Officer Course, Fort Bliss, 1972.

Active Duty with MACS-6, MASS-1, (both MACG-28, 2nd MAW, Cherry Point, NC); Reserve Duty with MATCU-73, H&MS-49, MABS-49, MTU PA-52 (all MAG-49 at NAS, Willow Grove, PA).

Memorable experiences and achievements include OIC, DASC Det., 32nd MAU, US 6th Fleet; CO of MATCU-73, MAG-49; two Mediterranean cruises, one north Atlantic cruise.

His military awards include the Marine Corps Reserve Medal, Armed Forces Reserve Medal, several letters of commendation/appreciation, National Defense Service Medal.

Currently he is a FBI special agent. He is married to the former Suzanne M. Ludlum.

PAUL LOSCHIAVO, Colonel, born June 14, 1954 in Brooklyn, NY. He was commissioned through OCS in 1976 and served with Comm. Sqdn. 29 before reporting to flight school in 1978.

Joining HMM-264 in 1980, he participated in two Med. Floats including one to Beirut in 1983. Then he served as XO of MABS-26, FAC with 2nd ANGLICO, and an instructor pilot with HMT-204.

Leaving active duty in 1988, he joined 4th ANGLICO, USMCR, where he served until 1996 as PltCdr., XO, and CO.

He is a graduate of the USMCR C&SC and the US Army War College. His education includes a bachelor's degree from Lehigh University and a master's degree from Pepperdine.

His decorations include the Meritorious Service Medal, Air Medal, two Navy Commendation Medals and a Navy Achievement Medal. He also wears the Naval Aviator Wings and Parachute Wings.

He is a vice president and branch manager with Merrill Lynch in Florida.

GARY L. LUMPKIN, Colonel, born July 2, 1946 in Wichita Falls, TX., lifelong resident of OK. Commissioned through PLC program May 24, 1968. Initially assigned communications MOS and served 18 months in Vietnam with units of 1st MAW. Subsequently  cross trained and served in infantry, artillery and JAG billets during 30 year career in USMCR.

Retired June 1998 while serving as one of two reserve officer judges assigned to Navy-Marine Corps Court of Criminal Appeals. Awarded Meritorious Service Medal, Navy Commendation Medal, Navy Achievement Medal

w/V together with other campaign and service awards.

Education includes BS from Southwestern Oklahoma State University and JD from University of Oklahoma.

Currently serves as vice presiding judge, The Oklahoma Court of Criminal Appeals, the supreme court for criminal cases in the State of Oklahoma.

EDWARD M. MANNING, Lieutenant Colonel, born July 22, 1931 in Pasadena, CA. Entered flight school as a Naval Cadet in September 1952. Assigned to VMF-323 and later VMF-223 at El Toro in 1954-55. He participated in Operation Desert Rock IV in the Mojave Desert in 1954. Spent 19 months in Japan, Korea and Okinawa, primarily with MAG-11.

Returning to CONUS in 1956, received a BS degree in aero engineering and took a position as engineering test pilot with Northrop Corp. in 1959. He spent six years with NAA and MDC as a research engineer and company astronaut on the Apollo and Skylab programs.

Upon retirement from active duty in 1957, he spent 18 years in the Active Marine Reserve with VMA-134 and VMO-8, flying the F9F, TV-2, A4 and OV-10. As operations officer for VMO-10, he was the first reserve pilot to fly the newly acquired OV-10.

In 1969 he joined MDC commercial division as a marketing manager and later as project manager on the MD-80. He retired from MDC in 1992 with 26 years of service, after which he built his retirement home in Fallbrook, CA, where he has a small lemon ranch.

STEVEN J. MARIETTI, Captain, born Aug. 27, 1966 in Kansas City, MO. Training: Summers of 1988-89, OCS, Quantico, VA; November 1989-May 1990, TBS; August-November 1990, Communication School,

Quantico, VA. Served with 9th Communication Bn.

Memorable experiences and achievements include Gulf War, Desert Shield/Storm, Somalia.

His military awards include the Navy Commendation Medal, Kuwait Liberation Medal.

Currently he is the deputy district attorney for San Diego County, CA.

He has been married four years and has one child.

DONALD E. MAROUSEK, Colonel, born Oct. 11, 1920 in Bronx, NY. Graduated high school 1938 and college 1942.

Enlisted Navy V-5 Flight Training Program, 1942, commissioned 2nd Lt., USMCR, February 1944 and ordered to Instrument Flight Instructor's School in Atlanta, GA.

He returned to Pensacola, NAS Whiting Field for 15 months as instructor in the Training Command and was then ordered to Opa Locka NAS for TBF familiarization and CQ, then to MCAS El Toro, and assigned to SS-46. He was released to inactive duty February 1946.

He joined VMF-232, Floyd Bennett Field and progressed from TBF to F6F and then F4U. His squadron was reactivated September 1950 for Korean conflict and deployed to El Toro where delays prompted orders to LSO School, Pensacola, where he flew F8F Bearcats and AD Marauders.

He returned to El Toro to join VMF-451, flying Corsairs and in April 1852 his squadron was deployed to MCAS Kaneohe Bay. He was transferred to VMF-235 as LSO and squadron was ordered to "Operation Warmwind," an air-ground exercise in Alaska. In September 1952 he was again released to inactive duty.

He joined VMF-244 in Columbus, OH and flew F9F 2 and 4 Panthers, F9F

6 and 8 Cougars and FJ 2 Furys from 1952-59.

In July 1959 his family relocated to Los Angeles and he joined MARG-2 NAAS, Los Alamitos.

Early in 1962 he was selected as air officer, 12th Staff Group, Chavez Ravine where he generated operation orders for annual air-ground exercises at 29 Palms MCB.

He retired in July 1974.

LANDON C. MARTIN, Colonel, born July 12, 1924 near San Antonio at Charlotte, TX. He attended San Antonio Junior College 1941-42 and enlisted in Naval Aviation Flight Training in December 1942. At age 19, In June 1944, he was commissioned a 2nd lieutenant, USMC, as a Naval Aviator at NAS Corpus Christi. After operational training in fighters at NAS Green Cove Springs, FL, he graduated from Naval Flight Instructors College, NAS New Orleans and was designated a naval flight instructor. He instructed flying at NAS Norman, OK and NAS Corpus Christi, 1944-46.

During 1947-48, he was a Corsair pilot in VMF-234, NAS North Island, San Diego, CA. He received a BA from the University of Arizona, Tucson in 1949. In 1950 he was designated an Air Force flight instructor, Craig AFB, Selma, AL and instructed Air Force cadets at Greenville AFB, Greenville, MS. In 1951 he was transferred to VMF-124 as a Hellcat pilot at NAS Memphis. He was later transferred to VMF (N)-531 "The Gray Ghosts", MCAS Cherry Point, NC as an all weather night fighter pilot, flying the F7F-3N, Grumman Tigercat. In July 1952 he was transferred to VMF (N)-513, "The Flying Nightmares" in Korea, flying combat in Tigercats. Beside being a night fighter pilot, he was the assistant intelligence officer of the Flying Nightmares. He was award the Distinguished Flying Cross and three Air Medals, during his tour of duty, July 1952-May 1953. Later in the Marine Corps Reserve, he was CO, VTU 8-26 (Intel), El Paso 1956-62; CO, 4th Recon Bn., San Antonio, TX 1965-68; CO, VTU 8-13 (S), San Antonio 1968-74.

He married Claire Gill (47 years in 1998) and has four daughters: Kathleen, Mary Ellen, Susan and Emee, and eight grandchildren.

He retired in 1974. He and his wife,

Claire, own Texas Land Exchange, Inc., San Antonio, a land development company.

FRANK G. MATTHEWS, Major, born Sept. 6, 1930 in Cynthiana, KY. Trained at Quantico, VA, and served with 1st MarDiv. in Korea, 1954; CO Lexington Reserve Unit, 1964-65; retired, Reserve Program, February 1974.

His military awards include the Korean Service Medal, United Nations National Defense and Reserve ribbons.

He is now retired and lives in Nicholasville, KY.

WILLIAM P. "BILL" MCCAHILL, Colonel, born June 29, 1916 in Marshaltown, IA. Training: PLC, 5th ROC, Quantico, VA; War College, DC, Sr. Reserve courses.

Active duty 1941-45; Reserves 1945-71. Served with Div. PR, HQMC, asst. dir., Quantico, 1942-43; MCB, San Diego; OIC, PR, FMF, 4th MarDiv.; PRD, 4th MarDiv., CINCPAC, Pearl Harbor, Guam, Sr. PRD.

Memorable experiences and achievements include serving as volunter exec. dir., MCROA, 1946-1952.

His awards include Legion of Merit, Non Combat, Marine Corps Medal, FMF, three Combat Area Stars (Saipan, Tinian, Roi-Namur), Theater Ribbons, Pre-Pearl Harbor, US and PAC.

Served as executive secretary on the President's Committee on the Handicapped for 23 years under Truman, Eisehower, Kennedy, Johnson and Nixon before retiring at the age of 82. Currently serves as a volunteer on the Board for the Handicapped.

He has three children: Mary, Bob and Bill; seven grandsons and one granddaughter. Son, Capt. Bob McCahill, USMC, was KIA, he received two Bronze Stars.

ED MCMAHON, Colonel, born March 6, 1923 in Detroit, MI. He received Wings andcommissioned a 2nd lieutenant at Pensacola on April 4, 1944. He took Corsair training and became an instructor and test pilot in Corsairs at Lee Field in Green Cove Springs, FL. He was called back to duty with the Marines in 1952 and flew 85 missions with VMO-6 in the Korean War. He was awarded six Air Medals.

He returned to television in 1953 and subsequently joined Johnny Carson for their historic 30 year run on The Tonight Show.

He has a BA in speech and drama from Catholic University of America in Washington, DC. He is president and founder of McMahon Communications, Inc. He is on the board of directors of the Marine Corps Scholarship Association, vice president of the MDA and vice president as well as a member of the board of directors of the Horatio Alger Association.

GERALD F. "JERRY" MERNA,

1st Lieutenant, born April 1, 1930 in New York, NY.

Enlisted April 1, 1947 and trained at Parris Island SC, Plt. 47, Naval Justice School, Newport, RI, June-August 1953; Instructor Orientation Course, 1955.

He served with the 22nd Marines, Quantico, VA, 1947-48, Force Troops, FM FLANT, Lejeune, NC; Korea, 1952-53.

His Korean service includes: Weapons Co., 1st Bn., 5th Marines; H&S Co., 1st Bn., 5th Marines; 1st MarDiv. HQ; Easy Co., 2nd Bn., 5th Marines.

His Vietnam service includes: 3rd MarDiv. HQ.

Memorable experiences and achievements include action as a platoon sergeant in one of the most bitter engagements of the war, Outpost VEGAS.

His military awards include two Navy Commendation Medals (w/Combat V), Korean Service Medal (w/3 stars), Korean Presidential Unit Citation, two National Defense Service Medals, United Nations Service Medal, Vietnamese Cross of Gallantry w/Bronze Star, Vietnamese Cross of Gallantry w/Palm (unit award), Vietnam Service Medal (w/2 stars), Presidential Unit Citation, Vietnam Campaign Medal (w/Device 1961), Good Conduct Medal (6th award), Combat Action Ribbon.

He is currently president, Merna and Associates in Potomac Falls, VA.

He has been married to Dorothy for 48 years and they have one son, one daughter, one granddaughter and two grandsons.

J. TODD MILES, Brigadier General,

Ret), born Aug. 21, 1950 in Springfield, MA. Commissioned in the PLC Program upon graduation from Springfield College in 1972, After TBS and Engineer School, he reported for service with 3rd Engr. Bn. in Okinawa. He took an engineer platoon "on float" with BLT 3/4. Upon return to CONUS, he commanded two platoons at OCS before release from active duty.

During his reserve career, he served with C Co., 1st Bn., 25th Marines, and later with MWSS-473 at NAS, South Weymouth. He served for a short time at MCAS, El Toro during Desert Shield. A few years after he retired he was offered a state commission in the Massachusetts Military Reserve. He currently commands 2nd Bde., MMR at Camp Edwards.

He is president of Zanadu, Inc., a land development company and Millbury Travel Service. He also teaches part time at Becker College.

ROBERT D. "ROB" MILLBERRY,

Lieutenant Colonel, born in 1946. Enlisted in 1967, San Diego. Cpl. Enlisted Commissioning Program, 52nd Special OCC, 1968. Regular (0302). Rifle and Weapons Plt. Cmdr., XO, and CO of B/1/6. Instructor, Leadership School, 2nd MarDiv., CLNC. Special Warfare School - Military Advisor/Vietnamese Language Course, Fort Bragg, NC. CO of A/1/9, director, 3rd MarDiv. Leadership School. Discharged Okinawa as captain, returned to CONUS via Trans-Siberian RR (1975).

Reserve (0302/0802/0402): CAX Umpire, 29 Palms; VTU-CA03; liaison officer, Camp Pendleton; OIC, Sacramento Marines (Motor Transport maintenance); XO of 5/14, Treasure Island; MTU-CA29; MILES operations/training officer for Desert Training-91; CO of MTU CA-03; combat watch commander, FMFPAC, Desert Shield; plans officer, 4th MarDiv., New Orleans.

Schools: Advanced Infantry Officer Course, Quantico; Artillery Officer Course; Intelligence Course, Little Creek; Staff Planning, Coronado; Air War College, Command and Staff College.

Past chapter president of MCROA and National Sojourners #133.

Currently a field representative for the California Department of Justice.

PAULL MICHAEL "MIKE" MITCHELL, Colonel, born Sept. 1, 1936 in Toledo, OH. Training: September 1959-June 1960, Quantico, VA.

Served with 1st Bn., 12th Marines, 3rd MarDiv.; CO, MTU In-1; MTU KY-3 (law); MDB Station KY-1

Awards include the Meritorious Service Medal, National Defense Service, Selected Marine Corps Reserve Medal and Armed Forces Reserve Medal.

He currently is an attorney. His father, E.A. Mitchell, was Cmdr. USNR, Frogman Co., WWII, Silver Star. RAdm. F. Paull Mitchell, USN (Ret), both deceased.

MICHAEL A. MOHLER, Lieutenant Colonel, born Jan. 10, 1950 in Astoria, OR. Enlisting in the USMC in 1968, he served with the 26th Marines in Vietnam from 1969-79. In 1977, he was commissioned a 2nd lieutenant and served with 7th Marines and the Ground Defense Force in Guantanamo Bay, Cuba. He left active duty as a Captain in 1984.

In December 1984 he joined 2nd Bn., 23rd Marines and filled several billets at the company and Bn. level. The Bn. was activated for Operation Desert Storm in December 1990 and was stationed in Okinawa until August 1991.

In June 1992, he joined the IMA Det. of the I MEF Command Element at Camp Pendleton, CA serving in the G-3. He deployed to the Middle East three times for Exercise Native Fury and was called to active duty on several occasions including Operations Restore Hope and United Shield. In June 1996, he assumed command of the Mobilization Training Battalion at the School of Infantry, Camp Pendleton, CA.

His education includes a BA from Texas Wesleyan University. His awards include the N&MCAM, Combat Action Ribbon, Good Conduct Medal and other campaign and unit awards.

Memorable Experiences: On one occasion during a night off in the battalion rear, one of the platoon machine gunners, Gray, had gone to the club and consumed a significant amount of alcohol. Upon his return to our hooch, he was met by another machine gunner who asked if he could throw a K-Bar between his feet. Gray reluctantly agreed stating, "Don't hit my foot because I'm going on R&R tomorrow." The second gunner threw the knife with a great deal of force, and as luck would have it, the knife hit Gray in the foot, going completely through, and sticking into the floor. Gray looked down and said, "Damn it, I told you not to do that!" Those of us in the hooch couldn't help but laugh. The knife was removed and Gray was taken to BAS for treatment. Happily, he went on R&R the next day.

On the first day of an operation on Barrier Island, the battalion found the area swarming with Viet Cong and took incoming all day. That night his squad (with attachments) were sent on an ambush. The first four Marines had just entered a tree line when all hell broke loose. There was automatic fire and mortar rounds hitting all around. Mohler happened to be "Tail End Charlie" that night so when the VC initiated the ambush, he thought the first four Marines had to be dead. As they moved up on line, he was relieved to find that no one in the squad was hurt. The next morning, however, after returning to their lines, they were told that a mortar round had killed one Marine when the VC hit the company perimeter. During this same operation an incident occurred which later seemed funny, but at the time scared the hell out of everyone. One of the members of my squad would sometimes "sleepwalk." On this particular occasion he had been sound asleep when he experienced one of his episodes. While still asleep he attacked one of the platoon machine gunners thinking he was a VC. This caused the unlucky gunner to let out a loud scream. Another machine gunner, thinking the unlucky gunner had been attacked, yelled out "They got Brown." The entire perimeter was instantly alert thinking the VC were inside our lines. It took several minutes before anyone discovered what really happened. The next morning word spread that Brown had been "attacked" and everyone, including Brown, had a good laugh.

He is presently employed as a deputy sheriff in Santa Barbara County, CA and resides in Lompoc with his wife, Susan. They have three children ages, 23, 20 and 19.

RONALD D. MOORE, Captain, born Oct. 16, 1939 in Madera, CA. Enlisted USMCR in 1957. Commissioned in 1966 through 40th OCC, he served as an infantry officer with the 1st MarDiv. in Vietnam, 1967-68, and the 3rd MarDiv. and 5th MarDiv. at Camp Pendleton. Served as platoon commander, executive officer, company commander and asst. S-3 of 3rd Marines and 28th Marines. Participated in three campaigns in Vietnam including Tet Offensive.

Graduate of Demolitions Course, Naval Justice, and Corrections. Awarded NUC, PUC, Combat Action Ribbon and campaign and other service medals.

He is a member of TROA, MCA, MCROA, and life member of VFW, DAV and American Legion. In 1990 he was honored for service with CA Criminal Justice Planning. Served as superintendent of schools for 23 years. Cited by CA State Supt. of Instruction for leadership and professionalism in education in 1999.

Education includes BA from CA State, Fresno; MA from USIU; and Ph.D. from CA Western. Presently a consultant for educational matters and a part-time university instructor. Wife, Shirley, is a former teacher. Oldest son, Ron, is a producer/writer with Paramount (Star Trek), youngest son, Mike, is a congressional liaison officer to the Australian Embassy.

JOSEPH M. "JOE" MORIN, Lieutenant Colonel, born Dec. 12, 1921 in Lowell, MA. Training: Chapel Hill, NC, Squantum, MA, Pensacola, FL, El Toro, CA.

Served with: VMF-225, Guam, VMF-216/217; Task Force 58, VMF-331, Pohang K-3, Korea. Carrier duty was a most rewarding experience.

Awards include the Distinguished Flying Cross and Air Medals.

He is retired and, after 49 years of marriage to Yvonne, became a widower in 1994. He has five children.

CHARLES T. MUSE SR, Colonel, born 1947 in Hamlet, NC. Commissioned through the OCC Program, Jan. 1, 1970. He served as the CO of "I" Co., BLT 3/4 as well as a Weapons Plt. Cmdr. and a Co. XO with 2/7.

Returning to CONUS in 1973 and to civilian life, he began a career in higher education as an instructor at Coastal Carolina Community College (CCCC). Obtaining a D.Ed. at North Carolina State University in 1978, he continued to teach at the University of

Nevada-Reno (UNR), obtained the rank of associate professor at Georgia Southwestern State University (GSW) and taught at MCSSS on the adjunct faculty for 10 years. He has held various leadership positions in higher education to include, assistant dean at UNR, director of continuing education at GSW, director of public services and advancement at GSW and vice president for academic affairs at Florence-Darlington Technical College (FDTC). He is an author and lecturer having contributed to three text books, published over 40 articles, and has made presentations at international, national, and state conferences.

Dr. Muse continued his service with the USMCR holding a command billet at each rank. He served with the 4th FSSG to include Plt. Cmdr. for Supply Co., CO of MSSG-45 and OIC SMU. He served as the OIC of H&MS-49 Det. and as the group supply officer for MAG-42. As the senior advisory to the non-resident program for Command & Staff College, he was the OpFor Cmdr. for five years. As a colonel he has served as the area commander for MCES and as the A C/S for RS, Marine Corps Recruiting Command. His decorations include, MSM, NCM, NDM, VSM, and 15 other Navy and Marine Corps awards.

In addition to his Ed.D., he has an AAS degree from CCCC, an AB degree from Catawba College and a MBA degree from East Tennessee State U. He has been very active in his professional life and community affairs receiving numerous awards and serving on various boards.

Dr. Muse married the former Susan Hutchins in 1975. They have three sons and reside in Florence, SC. He is currently the vice president for academic affairs at FDTC.

HARRIS J. "SKIP" NADLEY,

Captain, born July 6, 1926 in Philadelphia, PA. Training: Parris Island, 1944. Served with: 6th JASCO (Now ANGLICO); 6th MarDiv.; Naval War College.

Memorable experiences include Okinawa Campaign; being WIA, 1945; Occupation of China, 1946.

His awards include the Pacific Service, American Defense, Navy OCC, China Service, Reserve, WWII Victory and Good Conduct. He was econ. policy advisor to Mayor Frank L. Rizzo, Philadelphia, 1978; and regional VP, Naval War College Foundation, 1997.

Graduated University of Pennsylvania, BS, 1950; Harvard University, MBA, 1952. Currently senior partner, Michael Nadley Co., CPA, Philadelphia, PA.

He and his wife, Barbara Ann Malone, have three children, Beth, Amy and Adam.

DONALD G. NELSON, Captain,

born Nov. 4, 1942 in Short Hills, NJ. Trained at Quantico, VA, OBS, 1964; Fort Sill, Artillery Officers School, 1965.

Served with 2nd Bn., 1st Marines (Special Landing Force) Vietnam, 1965-66; 10th Marines (Landing Force-Mediterranean), 1967.

Memorable experiences and achievements include being elected mess president, Officers Basic School, 1964.

He is currently an investment banker specializing in mergers and acquisitions.

He and his wife, Lynn, have one son, Matt, who attends Northwestern University.

EDMUND A. NELSON, Major, born

June 16, 1920 in Hooperville, MD. Training: August 1942, NAS, Anacostia, DC; November 1942, Pensacola, FL; June 1943, Sanford, FL.

Units served with: VMJ-352, VMR-352, VMF-321.

Memorable experience was being the pilot on three round-trip flights in R5Cs from NAS Alameda, CA to MCAS Ewa, Oahu. He also made several flights as pilot in R5Cs carrying passengers and cargo from Ewa to South Pacific, Philippines, Central Pacific, China and Japan. During his career he flew the N3N, N2S, SNV, SNJ, SNB, P2Y, PBY, PV, R4D, R5C, F6F, F8F and AD.

He retired as vice president STEELTIN Can Corporation, a division of US Can Corp.

He and his wife, the former Anita Marguerite Ross, have a son, a daughter and six grandchildren.

STUART F. NELSON, Colonel,

born Feb. 10, 1925 in Minneapolis, MN. Commissioned in the V-5 program, he served with VMF-234 and VMF-215 before reporting to Korea in 1951. He flew 84 missions with the "Checkerboard" Sqdn., VMF-312, from K-18 and the USS *Bairoko,* CVE-115. He was recommended for the Silver Star, awarded the Distinguished Flying Cross, three Air Medals, and other campaign and commendation medals.

Returning to CONUS in 1952, he was employed by TWA where he flew DC-3s, 4s, M404s, Constellations, B707s L1011s and B747s in the domestic and international divisions. He spent two years in Saudi Arabia in Flight Operations Management. He continued his association with the Marine Corps, affiliating with several VMF-VMA squadrons, flying F8Fs, F9Fs, T-33s and A-4s. He commanded VMA-134, MABS-46, the 29th Staff Gp. and the 51st MAU. He attended staff courses at Quantico, Coronado, the Armed Forces Staff College, the Naval War College and the National War College.

In 1967 he participated in the Civic Action program in the Da Nang area. In 1971 he was elected national president of MCROA, and later was active in the initial formation of MCAA.

His education includes a BBA from the University of Minnesota, graduate study in economics at the University of Kansas City, and various business seminars. He is presently a distributor for the Avtek Corporation, and a member of its board of directors.

CHARLES M. NETTLES, Lieutenant Colonel, born March 14, 1923 in Montpelier, ID. WWII carrier pilot, VMF-221, USS *Bunkerhill*, covered Iwo Jima, Okinawa, 1st carrier raids on Japan; Korea, 1st Air and Naval Gunfire Liaison Co. (1st ANGLICO), forward air controller, KMC.

Retired in March 1966 with 21 years, eight months of service. His awards include the Distinguished Flying Cross, four Air Medals, Korean Service Medal w/2 stars and United Nations Service Medal.

Education: BS, Texas A&M; MS, University of Houston. He is a registered professional engineer in TX and chairman of Tex-Trude Inc., Channelview, TX.

He is married and has three children and five grandchildren.

CYRIL JOHN "CY" O'BRIEN, Captain, born Jan. 30, 1919 in St. John's, Newfoundland, Canada. Trained at Parris Island, Quantico, VA; Pendleton, Little River.

Served with 3rd MarDiv., Bougainville, E-2-3 (infantry); Guam, Iwo Jima division as combat correspondent.

Memorable experiences and achievements include assault landing, Guam, patrols and receiving the Navy Commendation Ribbon.

Currently he is a newspaperman.

GEORGE H. O'KELLY JR, Lieutenant Colonel, born May 4, 1942 in Florence, SC. Graduate of The Citadel, University of South Carolina School of Law and Naval Justice School. Military service includes MCAS Cherry Point, FLC, Republic of Vietnam, MCRD Parris Island. Reserve duties include XO, Co. "C, 4th LSB, Eastern Area Counsel's Office, CLNC, and IMADet, MCRD, Parris Island.

Military awards include Navy-Marine Achievement Medal, Combat Action Ribbon, Humanitarian Service Medal, Vietnam Service and Campaign Medals.

Practicing attorney in Beaufort, SC. Former municipal judge and city councilman for Beaufort. Chairman of Vietnam Veterans' Memorial in Beaufort, SC.

He is married to the former Yancey Heins and they have three sons.

RICHARD J. O'MELIA, Lieutenant Colonel, born May 24, 1917 in Rhinelander, WI. Joined USMCR in 1931, while attending Notre Dame; Quantico for PLC in 1937; San Diego, 1938; left law school in 1940 to enlist in Marine Corps Aviation. Trained at Glenview E Base  (first Marines to go there), January 1941; Pensacola, Miami, NAS fighter training. Made 2nd Lt., Dec. 4, 1941; instrument instructor, NAS Jacksonville and Miami NAS; Quantico, Bomber Sqdn. 332, Bogue Field, NC. Overseas: Midway, EWA, joined close air support group.

Memorable experiences and achievements include flying off USS *Natoma Bay*, Leyte Gulf landing, close air support landing, Iwo Jima and Okinawa (first time close support was run by Marines instead of Navy).

His awards include the Bronze Star for Valor (Iwo and Okinawa), Freedom Medal (Philippines), Presidential Unit (Philippines) and all the regular medals.

He had three brothers in service: one in USN, two in US Army (one after resigning as FBI agent). Richard is a retired attorney with 50 years of experience.

ROBERT E. PARCELL, Colonel, born Jan. 16, 1950 in Wooster, OH. Raised in Tucson, AZ and graduated Northern Arizona University in Flagstaff, AZ with a degree in forestry. He joined the US Forest Service and fought wildfires as a "groundpounder" for two years and as a smokejumper for four years.

In 1974 he attended the 90th OCS and graduated as 2nd Plt., Delta Co. honorman; finished in the top 10 percent

and augmented out of TBS. He served as rifle platoon and weapons platoon commander, Kilo Co., 3rd Bn., 5th Marines 3/5, assistant operations officer, 3/5, and XO, Lima Co., 3/5. In Okinawa, he served in the human affairs office, 3rd FSSG. While on the island he learned to scuba dive and made many 200'+ dives. He also obtained a master's degree in human resources management from Pepperdine University.

In 1979, he returned to the USFS Smokejumpers in Missoula, MT and completed a total of 120 parachute jumps after another four years. In 1982, he began a career in law enforcement with the Missoula County Sheriff's Department. After 17 years, he serves as the resident deputy in the Seeley-Swan. He lives with eight of his children and his wife, Danni. Two children from a previous marriage are grown up and on their own.

In the reserves, he served as forward observer, platoon commander, XO and commanding officer for Battery "A", 1/14 in Spokane, WA. Next, he joined 1/14 as liaison officer, then as S-1/Adjutant. In 1991, he was activated with 1/14 in support of Operation Desert Shield/Storm. During the activation he also participated in Exercise Battle Griffin in Norway. After deactivation, he joined the 23rd Marines as an assistant operations officer and then the TTECG, MCAGCC, 29 Palms, CA, as the IMA det. head/tactical exercise coordinator.

His law enforcement honors include: the Purple Heart Medal for being wounded while on duty, the Armed Action Medal for being involved in a gun battle in the line of duty, and the Life-Saving Ribbon for saving the life of a dying hunter. He was selected as the 1992 Local Law Enforcement Officer of the Year, and the 1993 Montana State Law Enforcement Officer of the year. On April 14, 1994, he received a Presidential Certificate of Commendation from President Clinton at the White House.

HOMER PAUL, Colonel, born Sept. 14, 1932 in Claremore, OK. Training: Quantico, VA, June-December 1954; Pusan, Korea, March-June 1955; Osan, Korea, June 1955-January 1956; Camp McGill, Japan, January-June 1956.

Units served with: 1st 90mm AAA Gun. Bn., 1st MarDiv.; 3rd Svc. Regt., 3rd MarDiv.

Memorable experiences and achievements include serving as OIC of detachment of 33 Marines; teaching AAA to South Koreans; being part of naval advisory group attached to US Army; stationed on K-55 USAF base; participated in NAVMARLEX; on Iwo Jima 1956.

Awards include Formal Letter of Appreciation from Republic of Korea Army, National Defense and Good Conduct.

Currently chairman, president, CEO and principal owner of Citizens Security Bank, Bixby, OK; asset of 116 million.

Married Ramona and has four children, three stepchildren and nine grandchildren. His brother, William G. Paul, is also a colonel (Ret) in the USMCR.

WARREN I. PAUL, CWO4, born Jan. 1, 1931 in Washington, DC. the son of a career Marine officer. After living in China and in several US locations and completing 3-1/2 years as a Rutgers University student, he enlisted in the USMC as a Regular in January 1951. After recruit training at  MCRD Parris Island, SC, and advanced training at Camp Pendleton, CA, he joined B Co., 1st Bn., 5th Marines, 1st MarDiv., in Korea in July 1951. 11 months later he returned to CONUS and served as a NAS Jacksonville, FL duty brig. warden until his honorable discharge as a sergeant in January 1954. In 1953 he has been awarded a Bronze Medal in the Southeastern Division Rifle Matches.

After receiving a BA (journalism) from Rutgers, he enlisted in the Marine Corps Reserve in August 1954. During the next 34 years he served in infantry and intelligence assignments (and once each as supply officer and assistant adjutant) with 4th MarDiv. Inf., tank, counterintelligence (CI), and artillery units and MACS-31 and HMH-772 of the 4th Marine Air Wing. In 1966, GySgt. Paul, then intelligence chief, 2nd Bn., 25th Marines, Garden City, NY was appointed a warrant officer. The following year the battalion newspaper, published by the

reservists he trained, was named 2nd best in the USMCR. In 1976, a CWO-4, he complete basic CI training at the US Army Intelligence Center and School, Fort Huachuca, AZ.

In 1987, as the S-2 of 5th Bn., 14th Marines, during 12 straight day of 95°-108° temperature annual training duty in the field at Fort Bliss, TX, since the intelligence section's personnel were not available, he trained two non-intelligence Marine Reservists so effectively that after 5/14 passed its Marine Corps Combat Readiness Evaluation Survey (MCCRES) the regular Marine evaluators specifically praised the section's performance as outstanding. The following year, at the age of 57, he commanded the 31st Interrogator-Translator team when it became one of the first Marine units to attend and complete the professionally demanding USAF Survival, Evasion, Resistance and Escape (SERE) course at Fairchild AFB, Spokane, WA.

In 1990 the 200-page Mobilization SOP he had completed before retiring in November 1988 effectively facilitated mobilization of Los Angeles, CA, Reserve Marines for the Gulf War, according to the Los Angeles USMCR units' assistant inspector-instructor.

CWO-4 Paul's military awards include the Navy Commendation Medal, US Presidential Unit Citation, Marine Corps Good Conduct Medal, Selected Marine Corps Reserve Medal w/seven stars, Armed Services Reserve Medal w/ Gold X Device, Korean PUC, National Defense Service Medal, USMCR Ribbon, Korean Service Medal w/4 stars and UN Service Medal.

He earned an MA (humanities) in 1966 from Newark State (now Kean) College (of NJ) and a Ph.D. (education curriculum; minor in communications and sociology) in 1972 from Ohio State University. His civilian occupations have included newspaper reporting and editing, corporate and banking public relations, civil service (Department of the Army Civilian), cable television producer and director, educational consultant, assistant director team member on such television shows as *The Love Boat, Hotel* and *Hell Town,* and full-time or adjunct professor at six universities. At present he is Director of Training (with rank of colonel), Premier Residential

Security USA, and Florida-licensed instructor, Premier Security School, Palm Beach Gardens, FL.

He is divorced and has two sons, one an attorney in Pennsylvania and the other, honorably discharged as sergeant after 8-1/2 years in the Regular and Reserve Marine Corps, the senior electrical engineer for the Ford Motor Co. plastics plant in Sandusky, OH.

CHARLES D. "GOOEY" PERRIGUEY JR., Lieutenant Colonel, born Feb. 15, 1945 in Glendale, CA. Enlisted in October 1965. Commissioned in the Enlisted Commissioning Program (ECP) after being accepted as a MarCad. Completed OCS and TBS before designation as Naval Aviator, August 1968. He flew the TH-13M and CH-34 and served with HMM-365, flying the CH46A, before reporting to Phu Bai, RVN in January 1969.

He flew over 540 combat missions in the UH-1E Huey with the "Scar Face" Sqdn., HML-367. Reassigned to HML-167, Marble Mountain, RVN. He also flew "Prairie Fire" missions as "Eagle Claw" and was attached to the "Magnificent Bastards", 2nd Bn., 4th Marines as forward air controller and air liaison officer. Controlled and trained team members in the control of all allied aviation assets employed in RVN, including A-1 SPADs, ARVN T-28s, Air Force (Night Owl), F-4s, F-8s, A-4s, A-6s (including TPQs) helo gunships, AC-47, AC-130, B-52, allied artillery and naval gunfire. Combat action in North and South Vietnam, Laos and Cambodia. He was awarded the Silver Star, Purple Heart, 27 Air Medals, Combat Action Ribbon, and eight other medals and ribbons.

Returning to CONUS in 1970 he was assigned to HMM-265 and HMM-163 flying the CH46D, D+ and F models. Attached to H&HS-3 (later MWHS-3 and was assigned to 3rd MAW staff and special projects officer, completing preliminary plans for the eventual acquisition of recreation facilities in the Big Bear Mountains and Camp Pendleton Beach. In 1971, he completed active duty and reported to HMM-764, MAG-46 for reserve duty. Attached to 3rd ANGLICO as FAC and ALO, including "Operation Deep Front" near Anchorage, AK in January 1985. Periodically attached for duty as a FAC/ALO at MCAGCC, 29 Palms. He was HMM Sqdn. safety, operations and XO, IMA maintenance and XO and Group NATOPS and safety officer. Designated NATOPS check pilot, instrument check pilot and flight leader in CH-46D+ and E. Attended Aviation Safety Officers Course and Command Safety Course at NPGS, Monterey, CA and Amphibious Warfare School at Quantico, VA.

Joined the LAPD in January 1972, transferred in 1975 to the LAPD Air Support Division and received numerous law enforcement awards over the years.

His education includes: Los Angeles State College, East Los Angeles College and Rio Hondo College. He is a life member of the Marine Corps Aviation Association and the Reserve Officers Association.

He and his wife, the former Betty Glenn Thomas, have two daughters, Glenda Marie Perriguey and Virginia Beth LaMontagne. He resides in Whittier, CA and remains employed with LAPD.

JOE W. PERRIN, Major, born Sept. 12, 1935 in Jefferson County, AL. Training: 1957, Quantico, VA and Tyndall AFB School, Panama City, FL; 1958-60, El Toro, CA, 1959 GCA School, Olathe, KS.

Units served with: 1954-57, Howitzer, Birmingham, AL Reserve; 1960-69, MACS-4, Atlanta, GA; 1969-76, GCA Unit, Memphis, TN (NAS Millington).

Memorable experiences and achievements include great memories of exciting weekends and summer camps.

He is currently a controller of a newspaper. He is married and has two sons.

GREGORY E. PHELPS, Major, born Jan. 2, 1944 in Spencer, IA. Training: OCS, Quantico, VA, 1967; commissioned Jan. 1, 1968; TBS, Motor Trans. Course, Camp Lejeune; Naval War College, RONO, 1983, Coronado.

Units served with: BG, 1st Bn., 3rd Marines, September 1968; 3rd Motor Trans. Bn., October-December 1968; 3rd Bn. 9th Marines, January-August 1969; CO, G Co., 24th Marines 75-7; 24th Marines 80-84.

Memorable experiences and achievements include embark. officer, 3rd Bn., 9th Marines upon withdrawal from Vietnam, Aug. 13, 1969.

His awards include the Navy Commendation Medal, CAR, Vietnamese Cross of Gallantry w/Palm, RUSM and NDSM.

He is currently a vocational rehabilitation counselor, IA Dept. for the Blind and has received the National Award for Job Placement of Disabled, 1986, state award, 1985.

He and his wife, Keiko, reside in Cedar Rapids, IA.

JACK NEWKIRK PHILLIPS, Colonel, born April 18, 1928 in Wichita, KS. Training: 1946-50, NROTC, University of Colorado at Boulder; 1950-51, Basic School, Quantico, VA; 1951-52, Camp Lejeune, NC.

Units served with: 1951-52, B Co., 1st Bn., 2nd Marines, 2nd MarDiv., CLNC; March-November 1952, H&S Co., 2nd Marines, 2nd MarDiv., CLNC; 1953-64, 1st 155 Gn. Bn., Den Co.; 1975-77, COVTU 9-7.

Memorable experiences and achievements include CO, 5th, 155, Gun Btry., FrTr., USMCR, COVTU 9-7, Reserves, commissioned officer mess golf champion, Quantico, 1951; president, MCROA Reserves, 1971-72.

Military awards received are National Defense Service Medal, OMCR Medal and MC Reserve Medal.

He is a retired financial consultant. He and his wife, Betty (retired med. tech), have three children.

ERIC NEIL PIPER, Colonel, born in Brighton, England. Training: After graduating from Adelphi University he spent four years on active duty and was assigned to Camp Pendleton in 1960. While on active duty he attended Basic School, Engineering School and served as engineering officer.

Units served with: 1st MarDiv., 26 years, Reserve, 4th MarDiv., CO of Co. B, Toledo, OH, 1968-70; CO of 4th Tank Bn., San Diego, CA, 1976-78.

He is the owner of a packaging business. He and his wife of 43 years, Beryl, have three children and three grandchildren.

FRANK R. POUND, Colonel, born Nov. 3, 1933 in Mayo, FL. Training: 1953-54, Pensacola, Corpus Christi, Cherry Point.

Units served with: VMA-121, MABS-12, VMF-144, VMA-142, BTU-IN, MTU-FL4.

Memorable experiences and achievements include BSJ, 1959; JD, 1961; University of Florida; moderator, National Defense University; lecturer, Florida Judicial College; chairman, Ti-Co. Airport Authority; Board of Governors, Flordia Bar; director, Valiant Air Command; Squadron CO for three tours.

He is a retired circuit judge. He has been married for 43 years and has four children and eight grandchildren.

TIMOTHY J. "TIM" QUINLAN, Colonel, born June 4, 1933 in Boston, MA. Enlisted in January 1953 as a member of a platoon leaders class. Upon graduation from Boston College in 1954 and The (officers) Basic School, he served his active duty with the Infantry Training Regiment, Camp Pendleton, CA, 1st Bn., 3rd Marines, 3rd MarDiv., FMF at Camp Fuji, Japan with tours as CO of H&S Co. and Battalion S-4 (embarkation officer). Following his release from active duty, he began his business career at Rexnord Inc., WI.

At the same time he began his reserve career as a platoon commander with the 16th Spec. Inf. Bn.; VTU 9-14; joined the 5th Communication Bn., Decemer 1963 in the Chicago area. Returned to Milwaukee in 1970 and rejoined the reserve establishment as XO of F Co., 2nd Bn., 24th Marines, 4th MarDiv. In 1975 he joined MTU 9-14 and in 1976 was selected as the CO of Detachment A, Wing Engineer Sqdn. 47, Green Bay, WI. In August 1979 he joined MACG 48 as Group S-4 and in September 1982 he was selected CO of MATCS 48 (Marine Air Control Group 48). In October 1984 appointed the OIC of the Mobilization Station in Milwaukee. In November 1986, selected as CO of the Marine Corps Mobilization Training Unit for Wisconsin. Currently he is a special staff officer in MTU KS-1, Kansas City and president of the MCROA, Milwaukee.

During his career, he has completed several advanced military schools: Landing Force Staff Planning, Air/Ground and MEB, command and Staff College and Amphibious Warfare School at Marine Corps School, MCB, Quantico, VA.

He is president of his own firm and a consultant with a human resource consulting firm. He is a certified compensation professional with the American Compensation Association. He is also a certified financial planner with International Board of Standards and Practices for Certified Financial Planners.

He has been married to M. Joan (Quinn) Quinlan for 42 years and has six children.

JERRY D. REECE, Colonel, a native of Scandia, KS, was born March 7, 1940. Commissioned through OCS, he served with the Brigade in Hawaii before reporting to Vietnam in 1965. There, as the assistant combat intelligence officer, G-2 Section, 3rd Div., he was charged with the task of maintenance of the daily (enemy) situation at the Da Nang, Chu Lai and Hue Phu Bai Enclaves. Returning to CONUS in 1966, he was assigned to the Marine Corps Recruit Depot, San Diego, as a Series Commander before release from active duty.

Col. Reece worked for Phillips Petroleum Co. in sales before joining Kroh Brothers Realty Co., Kansas City, in 1970. He was promoted through various management positions and was the executive vice president, residential division, when in 1987, he formed J.D. Reece Realtors by purchasing the residential arm of Kroh Brothers. Today he is the CEO of J.D. Reece Realtors and a director of J.D. Reece Mortgage. He was recently appointed by Governor Graves of Kansas to serve a four-year term as a member of the Kansas Real Estate Commission.

After leaving active duty, Col. Reece continued his association with the USMC. He affiliated with the 24th Marine Regt., Kansas City, where he served as a Headquarters Company Commander, S-2, and ultimately commanded the 3rd Bn. in St. Louis. He received a three-time appointment to the Secretary of the Navy's Marine Corps Reserve Policy Board at the Pentagon. As his last assignment, he assumed command of Mobilization Training Unit Kansas 01, USMCR Support Cmd., Overland Park, KS. He is a graduate of the Militia Command and Staff Course, Canadian Land Forces Cmd. and Staff College. He is presently a trustee of the USMCR Officers Foundation. His decorations include the Legion of Merit, Navy Commendation Medal w/Combat and the Combat Action Ribbon.

He is a graduate of the University of Oregon with a BS in finance. He and his wife, the former Patricia Karen Thomson of Duncan, OK, reside in Mission Hills, KS. They have three grown children and one grandson.

J. ANDREW "ANDY" RICE SR, Lieutenant Colonel, born May 22, 1960 in Fayetteville, NC. Commissioned in the PLC program, he finished first in his AI class at Pensacola. He completed flight training at Corpus Christi and Meridian. After receiving his wings in 1985, he flew the OV-10 at Camp Pendleton. He served as an instructor pilot at the USAF OV-10 Replacement Training Unit at Patrick AFB and Davis-Monthan AFB. He left active duty in February 1990. In the SMCR, he has served in VMO-4, MASD Andrews AFB, and MWSS-472.

He was selected to his present grade in June 1999.

He is a 1982 graduate of North Carolina State University, with a BA in political science. He is a pilot for Delta Air Lines and currently a first officer on the Boeing 767.

Married Kathryn (Taffy) Wells Rice and they have three children: Drew, Kathryn and Will.

JEFFERY RICHARDSON, Lieutenant Colonel, born May 10, 1958 in Warwick, RI. Training: 1985, TBS, Naval Justice School.

Units served with: 1985-89, 1st FSSG, Camp Pendleton; 1989-91, Naval Legal Service Office, Newport, RI; 1991-93, 6th MT Bn., 1994-98, Naval Justice School.

Memorable experiences and achievements include being CO, General Support Co., 6th MT Bn.

His awards include the Navy Achievement Award, National Defense, MVC, Expert Pistol and Rifle.

He is currently an attorney and is married with three children.

GEORGE A. "ART" RILLING, Colonel, born June 23 1928 in San Antonio, TX. Joined the Platoon Leaders Class in 1946 and attended two sessions in Quantico, VA. Commissioned a 2nd Lt. upon graduation, he was called up in 1950 to attend The Basic School then went to Korea as an artillery FO, returning in 1952 to Camp Pendleton until release in late 1952. He returned to civilian life and the reserve program.

In 1956 he returned to active duty in the reserve program. Stationed in Atlanta at 6th District HQ, he ran the VTU program until 1962 when he again returned to civilian life, started a business and rejoined the Reserves, serving in a number of billets in the FSR. He retired in 1988 with 43 years of service and continued to manage the Yellow River Game Ranch.

JOHN W. "ROBBY" ROBERTSON, CWO3, born in Camden NJ. Training: Philadelphia Navy Yard, 1963 (Basic Training USN).

Units served with: DD-702, USS *Hank*; VXE-6 Antarctical Support Sqdn., 1965-69; USN, VP-66, Willow Grove, 1983; MAG-49, USMC; MAG-11, Desert Storm, targeting officer, NMITC, USMC, VA BCH, VA.

Memorable experiences and achievements include being an aerial photographer in Antarctica on a mapping mission, a glacier was named the "Robertson Glacier" for his work there; being targeting officer MAG-11, Desert Storm. He worked more than 7,000 missions as targeting officer.

His awards include the Navy Achievement Medal (three awards), Combat Action Ribbon; Humanitarian Medal, National Defense (two awards), Antarctic Service Medal, KLM, USN and USMCR Good Conduct, various campaign ribbons.

He and his wife, Elizabeth, have no children.

THEODORE C. "TED" ROBINSON III, Colonel, born May 9, 1944 in Cleveland, OH. Training: OCS, Quantico; commissioned Nov. 10, 1966; Pensacola, Wings, January 1968.

Units served with were VMO-5 (HML-267); HML-367, RVN, April 1968-May 1969; VMO-1, June 1969-December 1970; Reserve: VMO-4, March 1971-82; H&MS-41, 1982-86 (CO, 1985-86); HQMC, 1986-1992, APP, ASM, MWR. Memorable experience was his high time as OV-10 pilot.

His awards include the Bronze Star w/V, Air Medal, S/F Air Medals (29 awards), Purple Heart, RVN Cross of Gallantry.

He is the president/CEO of Private Club Associates, Inc. Married to the former Mary Donnelly of Greenville, SC, and has two daughters, Kathy and Emily.

THOMAS M. RODGERS JR, Lieutenant jg, born Feb. 10, 1923 in Harrisburg, PA. Training: Navy V-12 Program; Navy CEC Midshipman School, Camp Pendleton, VA; CB Officers Training, Camp Endicott, RI.

Units Served with: 103 Naval Construction Bn.; Marine Corps Div. Station, Ewa, Oahu, Hawaii; 2nd MarDiv., Saipan and Okinawa; 10th Naval Construction Brigade HQ, Okinawa.

Memorable experiences and achievements include original combat landing at Okinawa with 2nd MarDiv., Minetoga and Hagushi beaches.

Military Awards: Combat Battle Star for Okinawa campaign.

He is currently a semi-retired petroleum engineer, attorney and MBA practitioner. He has a BS in petroleum engineering (Pitt); MBA (Tulane); JD (Loyola). He has been a member of the American Legion for over 50 years. Life member of MCA, MCROA, 2nd MarDiv. Assn., Marine Corps Historical Assn.

He is married with children and grandchildren.

WILIAM FORD LAW "WILL" RODGERS, Major, born June 28, 1960 in Winchester, MA. Training: OCS, 1980-81; TBS, 1986; NJS, 1987. Served with: 1st FSSG (LSSS); NMARA; HQMC.

His awards include Navy Achievement Medal, Military Outstanding Volunteer Medal, Armed Forces Reserve Medal, Selected Reserve Medal w/star, National Defense Medal.

He is an attorney and is active in local politics and currently serving on Newtown Legislative Council and board of trustees, Newtown Historical Society. He and his wife, Moira, have one daughter, Amelia.

ALFRED M. "OWL" ROME, CWO5, born April 23, 1936 in Memphis, TN. Training: NAS, Memphis, Cherry Point MCAS, 1954-55; El Toro MCAS, 1956-57; Yuma MCAAS, 1958-59; NAS RSY RDS P.R.

Units served with: VMF-124, VMA-124, MABS-42, MALS-41, 1 MEF, MARFOR SWA.

Memorable experiences and achievements include CAX, Alpine Warrior, Red Flag, two NATO exercises in Denmark, Desert Storm.

Military awards received are Navy Comm. Medal, NUC, MUC, SMCRMED, National Defense Service Medal, SWA Service Medal, Sea Service Dep. Ribbon, Armed Forces Reserve Medal, Marine Corps Reserve Ribbon, Kuwait Liberation Medal (Saudi Arabia), Kuwait Liberation Medal (Kuwait).

Currently he operates a landscape design service. He is a retired district distribution electric systems design engineer. He is a member of the execu-tive board of Harbor House (substance abuse rehab. center) and has been a member of MCROA since 1969.

He and his wife, Betty Ross Rome, have one daughter, Tia Renée.

ROBERT WARREN RUST, Colonel, born Aug. 16, 1928 in Jamaica, NY. Training: First Special Basic Course, October-December 1950, Quantico VA; Naval War College, Newport, RI, 1951.

Units served with: Dog Co., Charlie Co., 2nd Amphibian Tractor Bn., 4th Amphibian Tractor Bn., West Palm Beach, FL, VMF-142, Opalocka, FL.

Awards/achievements: Marine Corps Reserve Ribbon; Award of Merit for assisting in preventing assassination of Pres. of US, Sec. of Treasury and Chief US Secret Service, 1964; Outstanding Legislator award St. Petersburg Times, 1967, National Conference of the Fraternal Order of Police Award, 1967; Federal Criminal Investigators Assn. Award, 1977.

He is a semi-retired criminal prosecutor. His wife, the former Mary Ruth Duncan, passed away in August 1981. He married Theresa Maria Nagymihaly Dec. 18, 1982. He has six children: Benjamin, Lani, Debra, Bonnie, Randall and Wendy, and one stepchild, Brandon.

S. PAUL "SP" RYAN, Captain, born May 25, 1945 in Providence, RI. Training: Quantico, PLC, 1964-65; Basic School, 1966.

Units served with: 3rd Bn., 11th Marines, 1st MarDiv., MACS-1, MCAS Yuma; 10th Motor Trans. Bn., 4th MarDiv.

Memorable experiences and achievements include serving on Marine Corps Dinner Committee, RI, 1983.

Military Awards: Combat Action Award, PVC, HUC, Vietnam Ribbons.

Currently he is an attorney, self employed, environmental/land use. He was a probate judge from 1984-89.

He has five children: Heather, Tara, Berdine, Lacie and Jarrod.

WES SANTEE, Colonel, born in Ashland, KS (1932) and grew up on a cattle ranch near Ashland. He attended school in Ashland and graduated from the University of Kansas with a BS degree in education in 1954. While attending the university he attained national and international fame in track.

Some of his many awards are being named to the All-American team from 1951-56 by several organizations, received the Helms Hall of Fame "Athlete of North America" award for 1953, held the world record for the 1500 meters; and was also the 1953 national cross-country champion.

Attended Basic School, Quantico, VA, 1955-56; assigned to School Dem Troops, Quantico, 1956-57; transferred to Reserves in 1957. Assigned to VMF-215 Ftr. Sqdn., Navy Olathe, KS as S-2 officer and became CO of MATCU 72, Navy Olathe, KS. Assigned to Staff Group 22; CO 24th MarRegt KC MO; assigned back to Staff Group 22. Retired from Reserves in 1986.

Life member of MCROA, ROA and Navy League. Active in MCROA for 25 years, holding offices of Chapter president, 9th District director, national counsel, national president and board of directors. Also Navy VP for the Navy Section, ROA and chairman of ROTC Committee.

When he returned to civilian life, he established an insurance office in Lawrence, KS where he was actively engaged until retiring in 1990. He does a lot of public speaking, is active in community affairs member of the Presbyterian Church, Masonic Lodges, Shrine, Chamber of Commerce, American Legion, Optimist Club and has an interest in state and national politics. He is chairman of the board of trustees for the State of Kansas Sports Hall of Fame, located in Abilene, KS, and has directed the Toys for Tots Program in KS for over 20 years.

Col. Santee has been cited by Presidents Eisenhower and Johnson for his work in physical fitness and received the Navy Medal of Commendation in 1963 following his selection as one of the 12 top leaders in physical fitness in the US.

He is married to the former Marilyn Treadway from McCune, KS and they have four children, eight grandchildren and have homes in Kansas and Arizona.

ALBERT J. SATTLER JR, Colonel, born May 9, 1936 in Bronx, NY. Training: Quantico, VA, September 1959-August 1960; Basic School, January 1960; Comm. O Orientation CRS.

Units served with: MABS-17, MWSG-17, 1st MAW; 8th Comm. Bn., HQ Co., Force Troops Lant.; F/2/25; 6th Comm. Bn.; Det. 2, 2nd MAU; RAU, FMFLANT; REDCOM-2, USNR.

Memorable experiences and achievements include Iona College, 1958 (Magna Cum Laude); Fordham Law School, 1965; US Army War College CSC, 1985.

Currently an attorney, he and his wife, Magdalena, have five daughters.

GERALD DAVIS "GERRY" SCHMIDT, Colonel, born Sept. 24, 1918 in Dayton, KY. Training: 1938-42, University of Wisconsin ROTC; 1942, Marine Corps Schools, Quantico VA.

Units served with: (WWII) 6th MarDiv.; (Korea) 2nd Replacement Draft, Camp Pendleton, CA; (Vietnam) HQMC, Washington, DC, CO of Tank Bn. 4th, 1959-63, CA.

Memorable experiences and achievements include landing on Okinawa on Easter Sunday, and his two friends, John and Ed, he will never forget.

His awards include the Presidential Unit Citation, Navy Unit Commendation, Organized MC Reserve Medal, Asiatic-Pacific Campaign Medal w/3 Bronze Stars, WWII Victory Medal, National Defense Service Medal w/Bronze Star, Korean Service Medal w/Bronze Star, Vietnam Service Medal and the MC Reserve Ribbon.

Col. Schmidt is retired and an active member of S.D. Rowing Club.

He and his wife, Winnis, have two sons, Gerald II and Lance and one grandson, Gerald III. His father, Gerhardt, served in WWI in the Army, Archangel, Russia.

JOHN B. SHALLENBERGER, 1st Lieutenant, born April 10, 1917. Commissioned in 1943, graduating first in his class at Platoon Commanders School, Quantico VA.

He served as engineering officer, Air Base Group 2, first as NAS, Memphis, TN, then NAS, Coronado, CA, and finally at USMC Air Station, El Toro CA.

Education includes: The Hill School, Pottstown, Pa; Stanford University, BS in Engineering; Harvard University Graduate School of Business Administration, MBA; University of Munich, Germany.

Other achievements: Traveled to 120 countries of the world for Ford Foundation studying the degree with which each of the 120 nations' businesses had adopted scientific management techniques, culminating in *The Shallenberger Report,* delivered in 1951 in Sydney, Australia to the International Committee for Scientific Management. He serve as CEO for three corporations and retired as a Christian missionary to Mexico.

Anecdote: When I climbed aboard a transport aircraft carrying a bunch of Marines on weekend pass from San Diego to Los Angeles, the pilot called back, "Hey, Lieutenant, come up here and sit in the office, I don't have a copilot." As we were flying along, I noticed that the pilot was hung over and dozing off from time to time, and I asked, "Major, what do I do to land this thing if you pass out?" To which he replied, "Just do a wheels-up landing in the shallow water down there." I said, "But major, I'd kill thousands of people swimming down there!"

The major pointed back to the passenger cabin, and said, "But these are Marines!"

JOHN A. SHANAHAN, Lieutenant Colonel, Platoon Leaders Class, MCRD, Parris Island, SC, June-August 1952; Camp Goetche, VA, June-August 1953; Basic Officers School, Quantico, VA, June 1955; infantry platoon leader, 2nd MarDiv., Camp Lejeune and Vieques, PR, 1956; Embarkation School, Little Creek, VA, May 1956; company training officer, MCRTC, Parris Island, SC, 1956-57.

He served in Reserve Volunteer Public Affairs Unit, NY, 1960-81; is a past president of NY chapter of Marine Corps Combat Correspondents; past commandant of North Shore Queens (NY) Detachment of Marine Corps league; active with Marine Corps Scholarship Foundation from its beginning in 1962; and edited Leatherneck Ball journal, 1999.

A reporter for The Associated Press (Ret), he covered politics and city hall and is former president of The Inner Circle reporters group and past president of The New York Press Club. Currently, president of The New York Press Club Foundation.

DAVID F. SHEEHAN, Colonel, born July 28, 1933 in Easton, MA. Commissioned June 1955 via the PLC program. His active duty was with VMF (AW)-115 at MCAS, El Toro as squadron material officer. On release from active duty he joined VMF-214 at NAS, Los Alamotos. Upon formation of MAG-46 he moved to H&HS-46, where he was part of a supply officer cadre for 4th MAW. He performed his annual active duty in his mobilization billet of group supply office for either MAG-42 or MAG-46. Upon making LtCol. He joined the staff of 4th MAW in New Orleans, first as WSO, then G-4 and finally as deputy COS. During Mobilization Exercise Proud Saber he became the acting COS, the first (and probably only) non aviator to hold this position.

He then joined MTU CA-53 at NAB Coronado. He commanded the unit the last year before his retirement in June 1995. His personal decorations include the Meritorious Service Medal.

His education includes a BS in chemistry from Boston College and a MBA from UCLA. He worked for over 35 years for Rocketdyne Division of Rockwell International. Starting as a research engineer, then a senior financial advisor and finally as an executive advisor and division ombudsman investigator for fraud, waste and abuse.

Now retired, he lives on the beach in Port Huememe, CA and enjoys frequent international travel often leading small groups.

CHARLES "CHUCK" SHERWOOD III, Major, born Sept. 19, 1941 in Waterbury, CT. Training: TBS, August 1964-February 1965, Reserve Training, Amphibious Warfare, Command and Staff, Landing Force Planning (Div. level), San Diego.

Units served with: Active: 3/9/2/9 attached to 3rd Marines, 1st Marines. Reserve: 4th Div., 2nd Div. Foreign service: Irish Guards, Philippine Marines, 10th Ghurka Rifles.

Memorable experiences and achievements include cross cultural experience of living in Asia and dealing with a variety of ethnic groups and military organizations.

Military Awards: Bronze Star (V), Purple Heart, Expeditionary Medal (was first battalion to land in Vietnam, March 1965).

Currently he is an international financial and management consultant specializing in banking. He is married and has one daughter and one granddaughter.

FRANCIS J. SINCOX JR, Captain, born May 11, 1932 in Saginaw, MI. Graduated Emory University, Atlanta, GA with a BA degree in 1954 and MD degree in 1958. Entered USNR PEBD June 11, 1954, became SELRES in 1955 at old NAS Atlanta (now PDK airport). First flight in a Navy aircraft was there, in 1955, the station aircraft being an SNJ. Also there were SNB, P2V and AD-5. Duty there was with AWS-67.

Active duty USNR, 1957-58 at Emory University. Augmented to USN 1958-63. Duty at USNH, St. Albans, NY, sea duty with CVSG-58 aboard USS *Randolph* (Essex Class) CVS-15 with HS-10, VS-26, VS-36 and VAW-12 aboard. Experiences there included recovery of Mercury astronauts, Cuban Missile Crises, fire at sea, and collision at sea. Shore duty NAS Norfolk until 1963. Designated naval fight surgeon in 1958.

Transferred to USNR inactive, 1963-89, became SELRES again in 1989 at NMCTC, Charlotte, NC, missed the air side, and transferred in June 1990 to NAS ATL HMA-773. Mobilized for Persian Gulf War, November 1990-May 1991. Experiences there included mine strike aboard USS *Tripoli* LPH-10. Transferred to retire in May 1996.

Decorations include the Combat Action, Navy Unit Commendation Ribbon, Meritorious Unit Commendation Ribbon, FMF, Naval Expeditionary Medal, Armed Forces Service Medal, Armed Forces Expeditionary Medal, Naval Reserve Medal, Southwest Asia, Sea Service, Kuwait Liberation (Saudi), Kuwait Liberation (Kuwait), Expert Rifle and Expert Pistol.

Continues to be a member of NRA and MCROA. Resides in Gastonia, NC with wife, Joyce. Still practices medicine, part-time.

FREDERICK J. SMITH III, Colonel, born July 6, 1938 in Haverhill, MA. Commissioned via Officer Candidate

School in December 1964, he retired in May 1993 following 34 years enlisted and commissioned service. He served in a variety of command and staff billets ranging from platoon commander in an infantry company to deputy commander, 4th Force Service Support Group, FMF, USMCR.

Col. Smith's military schools include The Basic School, Defense Language Institute (LAO), Amphibious Warfare School, and the Canadian Forces Militia Command and Staff Course. His civilian education includes a BS Ed from the State Teachers College in Salem, MA and an M Ed from the University of New Hampshire.

Col. Smith's decorations include the Legion of Merit, Navy Achievement Medal w/Combat V, Combat Action Ribbon and other campaign and service medals.

He is married to the former Carol Clark and they have five children: Erick, Christopher, Jeanne, Matthew and Allison.

KEITH A. SMITH, Lieutenant General, born Nov. 11, 1928 in Cheney, WA. He attended Washington State University, 1948-52, earning BS degree in agriculture.

Enlisted in the USMCR May 12, 1951; completed Basic School, Quantico, VA, January 1953, and reported for flight training at NAS, Pensacola, FL. Designated naval aviator, May 12, 1954, he reported for duty with Marine Night Fighter Sqdn. 542, MCAS, El Toro, CA; transferred to Marine Nighter Fighter Sqdn. 513 in Korea. The squadron was redeployed to NAS, Atsugi, Japan.

Transferred to First Air Naval Gunfire Liaison Co., Camp Smith, Hawaii, March 1956, and returned to civilian life in February 1957. He participated with Reserve Marine Fighter Sqdn. 216, Naval Air Reserve Facility, Spokane, WA and Marine Ftr. Sqdn. 541, NAS, Seattle, WA.

December 1960 he returned to active duty with the 2nd MAW, MCAS, Cherry Point, NC; served as XO, Marine Air Control Sqdn. 6 and later as S-4 officer, Marine Wing HQ Gp. 1. In February 1962 he was reassigned as OIC of the cadre designated to build the first East Coast Marine F-4B Sqdn.

During April 1965 as a member of the first Marine F-4B Sqdn. to see action in Vietnam, he flew 156 combat missions and was awarded five Flight Strike Air Medals, one Single Mission Air Medal and Navy Unit Commendation Medal.

Returning to the US in July 1965, he attended the Command and Staff College at Quantico and was assigned as Head, Technical Training Section, Office of the Deputy Chief of Staff for Aviation, HQMC.

In August 1969, assumed command of Marine Fighter Attack Sqdn. 542, participating in 389 combat missions. In February 1970 he assumed command of Marine Fighter Attack Sqdn. 323, at El Toro.

In June 1970 he served on the staff of the Commander in Chief, Pacific, as Plans Officer, SE Asia Plans and Policy Branch. In June 1972 was reassigned as Head, Aviation Weapons System Branch, FMF, Pacific, staff. He was promoted to colonel August 1972.

Attended Industrial College of the Armed Forces, 1773-74; reported to HQ MC as assistant deputy chief of staff for Requirements and Programs. Made BGen. May 12, 1976 and assumed duty as assistant deputy chief of staff for aviation.

Transferred in May 1977 to 1st MAW on Okinawa, serving as wing commander and commanding general, 9th Mar. Amphib. Bde. for Team Spirit Exercise in Korea. Assumed duty as commander, MC Air Bases, Eastern Area and Commanding General, MCAS, Cherry Point, NC, June 1968; advanced to major general April 1979; assigned duty as deputy cheif of staff for Requirements and Programs, HQ MC, Janaury 1980; duty as commanding general, 2nd MAW, FMF, Atlantic, MCAS, Cherry Point, June 1981; promoted to lieutenant general Aug. 28, 1984 with duty as Deputy Chief of Staff for Aviation, HQ MC, Washington, DC.

Personal decorations include Legion of Merit w/Combat V, Distinguished Flying Cross, Meritorious Service Medal, Air Medal w/2 Gold Stars and Numeral 26 and the Navy Commendation Medal.

He and his wife, Shirley, have nine children: Kelly, Timothy, Holly, Cynthia, Lynn, Thad, Tadgh, Tara and Vincent (a Marine captain KIA, Beirut, Lebanon, Oct. 23, 1983), and 12 grandchildren.

KIM EDWARD "KOBE" SMITH, Lieutenant Colonel, born Nov. 15, 1947 in Long Beach, CA. Entered PLC in 1967 being commissioned in November 1970.

Units served with: MAG-11, VMO-6 and HMH-462. Lateral move to the intelligence field in 1980. Reserve assignments included HMA-774 and 3rd ANGLICO. Other assignments included: G-2 sections of 2nd MarDiv., 1st FSSG, I-MEF, III MEF, MarForPac, US Forces Japan (1-2). He was recalled in 1987 for service with USFJ; in 1990 with I-MEF in Desert Shield/Storm; in 1993 for Operation Restore Democracy in the Caribbean; and in 1998 with III MEF in Okinawa and Korea.

Personal awards include Meritorious Service Medal, Joint Service Commendation Medal, Navy/Marine Corps Commendation Medal, Joint Meritorious Unit Award, Navy Unit Commendation, Navy Meritorious Unit Commendation.

Memorable experiences include being among first Marines sent to Saudi Arabia during Desert Shield and organizing and running various intelligence operations under the auspices of IMEF G-2 on the Saudi-Kuwait border area, 1990-91.

Education: BA, Occidental College; NA, University of Southern California; JD, Southwestern University School of Law; graduate of Los Angeles Sheriff's Academy.

After 20 years with the Los Angeles Sheriff's Dept., Lt. Col. Smith entered the Los Angeles Co. District Attorney's Officer where he currently works as a criminal trial lawyer assigned to central operations.

LELAND W. SMITH, Brigadier General, born Feb. 2, 1914 in Joplin, MO. Enlisted in USNR in Atlanta, GA, in 1934; transferred to the Organized Marine Corps Reserve, Augusta, GA, 1936; advanced to sergeant major, 19th MC Reserve Bn. and commissioned 2nd lieutenant while on AD, Navy Yard, Portsmouth, VA. When the Japanese attacked Dec. 7, 1941, he was assistant communications officer at the Marine Barracks, Parris Island, SC.

After completing several communications and radar schools, he was ordered to the Pacific Theater in August 1943 with Marine Air Gp. 13 based in American Samoa. As wing communications officer he served at American Samoa, Funafuti, Tarawa, Majuro and Kwajalein, Roi-Namur, Eniwetok, Guam, Tinian and Saipan.

His awards include the Bronze Star w/Combat V and Legion of Merit. Released from AD in 1946, he was recalled in 1950 and served as electronics officer for CGAirFMFPac at El Toro, CA until released again on June 30, 1952.

From 1952 to retirement in 1970, he commanded several Marine Air Reserve units, including Air Warning Sqdn. 15 in Atlanta, GA and volunteer reserve air groups at Anacostia, DC and Atlanta, GA. He was selected for flag rank in 1965 and received his star from the Commandant of Marine Corps in 1966.

Received BA and MA degrees from George Washington University. In his civilian position, he served as a financial management and budget officer for the National Center for Disease Control, USPHS, in Atlanta, GA. After retirement from both Marine Corps and US Civil Service in 1970, he resided for 22 years in ruarl Newton County, AR, participating in numerous local and area-wide civic and charitable organizations.

He is currently national president emeritus of the Quarter Century Wireless Association; presently national president of the Old Old Timers Club; chairman of a national scholarship fund; a fellow and former director in the Radio Club of America; Aa Shriner; secretary of his Masonic lodge and active in his church. Over 85 years old he continues to make military presentations and speak at Marine Corps birthday parties and functions.

He is married to the former Helen Doernenburg and resides in Harrison, AR. He has three sons by an earlier marriage.

STANLEY A. SMITH, Lieutenant Colonel, current president of the Gen. H.M. Smith Chapter of MCROA was born Jan. 9, 1944 in Washington, DC and presently resides in San Diego, CA. Graduated from Brent School, Philippines in 1961 and worked for USAID in Cambodia on the trans-jungle highway.

Completed Basic School in June 1966 and was assigned to USS *Oklahoma City*, the last of the "big-gun cruisers" in the US Navy. As XO of the Marine Detachment, his general quarters station was director officer for both gun mounts. Received Letter of Commendation in 1967 from Commander, First Fleet for a lifesaving attempt.

As a reservist he was CO, A Co., 4th Tank Bn., and communications officer of the Reserve Naval Construction Force where he was in charge of military training for all reserve seabees. As G-6A with the 1st Marine Expeditionary Force, his deployments included "Operation Bright Star 1987" to El Hamman, Egypt. Here, he was the liaison officer to the Arabian 10th Mechanized Bde.

In his civilian career he teaches finance and was a co-founder/operator of the Marine Merchant Bank in Saipan which introduced FHA home lending to the Marianas. As community service he edits a journal published by the Knights Templar which has a goal of assisting the homeless in this country.

ELVA BICE "FLANAGAN" SPENCER, Major, born June 6, 1907 in Wharton, NJ. Degree from Upsala College and taught school before enlisting in the USMC in April 1943. She was in first boot camp class in New River, NC. Attained rank of sergeant and taught free aerial gunnery at Cherry Point, MCAS, NC. Attended Officers School at Camp Lejeune, NC.

First duty station as an officer was El Toro, MCAS, Santa Ana, CA where she was a ground training officer. She served in Los Angeles at the 12th Reserve and Recruitment District, did much public information work (even kissed Charlie McCarthy) and rode on the Marine Corps float in the Rose Parade.

She transferred to Denver, CO as inspector instructor of a women's reserve disbursing platoon. While there, had contact with Mamie Eisenhower and still has three of her letters. Next duty was at Marine Corps Recruit Depot in San Diego, CA, in charge of the Women's Reserve Program.

Upon retirement from the Corps as major in 1963, she returned to teaching school. She is now retired from teaching and has become a charter member of the Women's Memorial Foundation (Women in Military Service for America).

ROBERT J. "BOB" STOLARK, Colonel, born Aug. 8, 1929 in Williston Park, NY. Training: PISC, 1951; Basic School, Quantico, VA 1951-52; and various reserve training billets.

Units Served With: 2nd Inf. Training Command, Camp Pendleton, CA, 1952-53; 7th Rifle Co. (Gulf Co.), USMCR and various VTUs.

Memorable experiences include being company commander, T&R Cmd. and 7th Rifle Co., USMCR.

His awards include the Meritorious Service Medal, Marine Corps Organized Reserve Medal w/star, Armed Forces Reserve Medal and National Defense Service Medal.

He is a retired Supreme Court Justice, state of New York. He and his wife, Marilyn, have six daughters: Sally, Donna, Lisa, Nancy, Barbara and Amy.

FLOYD H. STOWE II, Colonel, born April 3, 1945 in Ann Arbor, MI. Enlisted in USMC in November 1964. After completion of recruit training at Marine Corps Recruit Depot, San Diego, CA. PFC Stowe was assigned to Communication and Electronic Bn. Upon completion of Aviation Radar Repairman Course, Lance Corporal Stowe was assigned to Marine Corps Air Station, Cherry Point, NC. Completed OCS, 1969, and assigned to Marine Air Control Sqdn. 6, Marine Air Control Group 28, 2nd MAW, MCAS, Cherry Point, NC.

In May 1970, Col. Stowe was assigned to Marine Air Control Sqdn. 4 in Vietnam. Upon the squadron's return to CONUS, he was reassigned to HQ&HQ Sqdn. 18 in Da Nang where he served as embarkation officer.

In June 1971, he was released from active duty and joined the USMCR. While in the reserves, he attended East Carolina University graduating in May 1976. After graduation he taught math and physics at Havelock High School, Havelock, NC. Additionally, he was a plankowner and fire chief of the Township Six Volunteer Fire Department.

Col. Stowe returned to active duty in the Category 6 Program in January 1979. He was assigned to the 4th Marine Aircraft Wing in New Orleans, LA, serving as assistant operations officer. He was promoted to major in April 1979 and to lieutenant colonel in September 1984.

In July 1985, Col. Stowe was assigned to Marine Air Control Group 48, 4th Marine Aircraft Wing, NAS, Glenview, IL, serving as the operations officer. While at Glenview Col. Stowe

was instrumental in establishing CONUS wide data link training and assisted in the planning and execution of the air command and control exercise in Dugway, UT.

He returned to New Orleans in August 1990 and was assigned to the 3rd Marine Aircraft Wing as the deputy G-1; promoted to colonel, August 1990, and assumed the position of assistant chief of staff G-1 in February 1991; assumed the position of assistant chief of staff G-1 for Marine Forces Reserve on June 7, 1992.

His education includes a BS from East Carolina University, MA from Central Michigan University and a MS from Loyola University of New Orleans.

A list of his decorations and awards include Legion of Merit, Meritorious Service Medal, Navy Commendation Medal w/Combat V and two Gold Stars, Meritorious Unit Citation w/2 Bronze Stars, Marine Corps Good Conduct Medal, Select Marine Corps Reserve Medal w/ Bronze Star, Vietnam Campaign Medal w/2 Bronze Stars, Armed Forces Reserve Medal w/Hourglass, Vietnamese Cross of Gallantry w/Frame and Palm, Vietnamese Civil Action Medal First Class w/ Frame and Palm, Vietnamese Service Medal w/Device.

Col. Stowe is married to the former Mary Louise Dunkley of Roxboro, NC and has two sons, Floyd III and Richard.

W. DAVID SULLINS JR., Rear Admiral, born Aug. 3, 1942 in Athens, TN. Commissioned a lieutenant junior grade in the USN Medical Service Corps on April 1, 1966. Upon his release from active duty in December 1969, he continued his Naval Reserve career as an optometrist providing primary eye care.

Duty: 1982-85, health services support officer, 4th FSSG; 1985-86, CO, NR NAVHOSJAX-108; 1986-88, CO, 4th Med. Bn., 4th FSSG, 4th MarDiv.; 1988-89, executive assistant, OP-093R, NR OPNAV-093-106, the Pentagon; 1989-90, principal advisor, BUMED code 07, Bureau of Medicine and Surgery. He was selected for Flag 1989. He was deputy director, Medical Service Corps and assistant chief, BUMED 04 (logistics).

RAdm. Sullins retired in August 1996. Awards include Legion of Merit,

Meritorious Service Medal, Navy Commendation Medal and Fleet Marine Force Ribbon.

He was the first medical representative to MCROA; first MSC representative to the Navy Reserve Medical Dental Flag Council. Currently he is president of a professional corporation, Eyecare Clinics, PC of Athens, Madisonville and Etowah, and chief of eye services at Woods Memorial Hospital, Etowah, TN. He is past president, former chairman of the board of trustees of the American Optometric Association.

He is married to the former Leslie Methvin of Cookville, TN and has two sons, William David III and Stuart Andrew, both optometrists. He and his wife reside in Niota, TN.

CHARLES E. SWOPE, Colonel, born June 16, 1930 in West Chester, PA. Graduated from West Chester High School, Bucknell University, The School of Law of Washington and Lee University and the Judge Advocate School (ARASU).

He joined the USMCR in 1950 as a private. Training followed at Parris Island, SC and Basic School at Quantico, VA. Assigned to Tank School at Camp Lejeune, NC and his MOS became 1802. Participated in tank operations in the 2nd and 8th Tank Battalions. After the Korean Conflict, he continued in the USMCR. He was assigned as CO, XO of 8th Special Inf. Co. in Lynchburg, VA and then served with the 2nd Inf. Co. in Roanoke, VA. He was assigned as marine liaison officer for Virginia Military Institute for three years.

He completed Amphibious Warfare School, I and II, Command and Staff College, I and II, Landing Force Staff Planning (Div.), Advanced Planning Coarse (ARASU-2-27), and the reserve seminar at the Naval War College in Newport, RI.

Over the years he has had many commands, i.e. tank platoon and company commander, OIC of mobilization station (Philadelphia, PA) CO of MTU-DE1 Delaware and judge advocate generals corps assignments.

In 1983, Col. Swope was elected national president of the MCROA of the US. He was a member of the Marine Corps Scholarship Foundation and the National Committee to Restore Tun's Tavern. His awards include the Legion of Merit Medal, National Defense Medal, Navy Commendation Medal, National Defense Medal and Congressman's Medal (1981) for Merit.

In 1998 Col. Swope continues his military association as a blue and gold officer assigned to the USNA, Annapolis, MD. He has continued his legal and corporate professional responsibilities and has been elected chairman of the board and president of the First National Bank of West Chester, also chairman of the board and president of First West Chester Corp. of West Chester, PA. He is a member of the board of directors of Pennsylvania Bankers Assn.; Governors Economic Council, vice president; Chester County Bar Foundation, member of American Bankers Assn., American Bar Assn. and president of West Chester Foundation.

He resides with his wife, Stephanie, and son, Charles Jr., in West Chester, PA.

JOSEPH JOHN TAMULIS, Colonel, born Aug. 18, 1917 in Beloit, WI. Joined the USMC in April 1942. Was commissioned December 1942. Made four D-Day landings in 13 months with the 4th MarDiv. on the Pacific Islands of Roi-Namur, Saipan, Taiwan and Iwo Jima. He was heading to spearhead the landing on Kyushu, Japan when Truman dropped the atom bomb.

He was awarded a Letter of Commendation w/combat V, two Presidential Unit Citations and two Navy Unit Citations.

Called back for Korea and eventually was OIC of the Logistic Section of the USMC Ordnance School in Quantico,

VA. He remained in the USMCR and retired in 1977 as a full colonel.

Graduated Cum Laude in science, Beloit College. Received Bessner-Lindsay National SAE Fraternity award for scholastics and athletics. In September 1992 he was inducted into Beloit Historical Society Athletic Hall of Fame.

He spent 2-1/2 years at University of Wisconsin, Bio Chemistry Department as research assistant.

He worked for 25 years as the regional chemical division sales manager for Eagle Picher Industries, retiring in December 1987.

He married Mary Lou Stang of Burlington, WI on Christmas Eve 1942. They have three children, five grandchildren and four great-grandchildren. Mary Lou passed away in November 1997.

JOHN M. TARA Colonel, born Feb. 11, 1921 in Oakland, CA. Entered the USN on May 14, 1942 and was commissioned 2nd lieutenant USMCR, March 24, 1943.

Military stations and schools included NAS Corpus Christi, NAS Glenview, MCAS El Toro, MCAS Ewa, MCS Quantico and NAS Los Alamitos.

Overseas duty was with the VMSB-133, MAG-24 at the South Pacific. He participated in the battles/campaigns at Solomon Islands, Bismarck Archipelago and Philippine Islands.

Memorable experiences included mission flight leader; duty as CO of VMF-123; operations officer of MARG-2; and CO of VTU (AVN)-10.

Retired July 1, 1972. His medals and awards include the Distinguished Flying Cross, five Air Medals and Navy Unit Commendation. He belongs to the Retired USMC (Category III) and the MCROA.

Attended University of Southern California and received BS degree in engineering, Jan. 31, 1948. His last

employment was with Western Airlines where he was airline captain until his retirement. Currently he lives in Sandy, UT and enjoys skiing, fishing and coaching baseball.

He married Lois M. Coker on Jan. 26, 1946 and they have two children and three grandchildren.

LARRY S. TAYLOR, Major General, born March 28, 1941 in New York, NY. Units served with include HMM-264, HMM-263, 3rd Bn., 8th Marines, HML-765, HMA-773, 4th ANGLICO.

Memorable experiences and achievements include being senior Marine to complete Marine Corps Marathon in 1993 and 1995; receiving Distinguished Service Medal and Air Medal.

Currently he is a Boeing 747 captain with Northwest Airlines.

Other significant achievements: CO, HMA-773, 1980-82; CO, 4th ANGLICO, 1982-84; CG, 2nd MEB, 1992-93; CG, 4th MAW, 1993-96. Active in MCROA, National Executive Committee, ROA; fellow of Inter-University Seminar on Armed Forces and Society, member, USO Council of Georgia-Alumni, Reserve Forces Policy Board, active with Georgia Tech Alumni Association.

ROBERT D. TUKE, Captain, born Dec. 5, 1947 in Rochester, NY. Commissioned June 7, 1969, as a marine option officer from the NROTC program at the University of Virginia. He served with the 2nd Tank Bn., Camp Lejeune, before reporting to the 2nd Combined Action Group, Hoi An, Quang Nam Province, Vietnam. He served as XO and acting CO of Combined Action Co. 2-4, January-May 1971. He engaged in numerous ambushes

and other engagements while commanding six combined action platoons (CAPs). He was awarded a personal Cross of Gallantry w/Bronze Star by the Vietnamese and a Combat Action Ribbon, Navy Unit Commendation and Meritorious Unit Commendation.

After 2nd Combined Action Group stood down, 1st Lt. Tuke was assigned to 3rd Tank Bn., where he served as XO in Japan and Okinawa. Upon returning to the US, Lt. Tuke served at Marine Barracks, Fort Meade, MD, as part of the Marine detachment guarding the National Security Agency. At that post he served as a captain of the guard of the Fort McHenry Guard, a Marine silent drill team that drilled from the 1812 manual at Old Fort McHenry.

After resigning his regular commission, then Capt. Tuke served in the USMCR in Nashville, TN while attending law school at Vanderbilt University. He now is a member of his own law firm, Tuke, Yopp & Sweeney, in Nashville, TN. He served on the board of directors and as secretary of MCROA from May 1996-May 1999.

He and his wife, Susan, have two children, Andrew age 18 and Sarah age 15.

WAYNE L. TWITO, Lieutenant Colonel, born Feb. 7, 1920 in Grand, ND. September 1942, flight training, Corpus Christi, TX

Units served with: VMJ-353, VMJ-952, VMJ-252, VMR-152 and VMR-352.

His awards include the Distinguished Flying Cross, Air Medal and three Gold Stars.

He is a retired Northwest Airlines captain.

He and his wife, Margaret, WASP, WWII, have two sons, Randy (orthopedic surgeon, St. Paul, MN) and Robert (paster, Cedar Falls, IA).

CRAIG S. VANDEBERG, Lieutenant Colonel, born Sept. 3, 1953 in Neillsville, WI. Commissioned November

1975. Primary MOS: aviation supply. Secondary MOS: ground safety specialist.

Served as personnel services officer, MWHS-1, MCAS Iwakuni, Japan and as supply officer, MWHS-2, MCAS Cherry Point, NC, before leaving active duty in 1978.

Subsequent reserve duty included: supply officer, VMGR-234 and MTU-IL-1, NAS Glenview, IL; HQSVCCO, 2/24, Chicago, IL; MTU-CA-43, NAS Alameda and Oakland Army Base. Current billet is admin. officer, Coast Guard Island, Alameda, CA.

His awards include the Armed Forces Reserve Medal, National Defense Service Medal, Standby Marine Corps Reserve Medal, Meritorious Unit Commendation, Certificate of Commendation (Desert Storm) and Marine Corps Commendation Medal.

Professional military education: AWS, C&SC, MAGTF, CSS, ACE, MEB, RCNSC. Education: BS in biology, University of Wisconsin, Eau Claire; MBA in management, University of Wisconsin, Whitewater; MS in industry and technology, Northern Illinois University.

Presently he is senior personnel representative, Federal Express, Hayward, CA.

Achievements include Senior Professional Human Resources national accreditation, Certificates in Employee Relations Law and Mediation.

WALTER E. VARNER, CWO4, born Oct. 26, 1941 in Opelika, AL. Completed basic in June 1963, Parris Island, SC and enlisted Reserves, December 1963-67.

Served with: MCDEC, TBS, Quantico; CAX 10-82, 29 Palms, CA, 4th FSSG; 1st MAW, Team Spirit; 23rd Marines MCCRES, Camp Ripley; MCMW Training Center, Bridgeport; CAX 8-86, 29 Palms, CA, 4th FSSG; Staff Planning, CSS LS Crs, NAB, Coronado; JCS Mobilization Exercise, "Proud Scout", PP&O HQMC; JCS WINTEX CIMEX (NATO) PP&O HQMC; JCS Exercise No-Notice Interoperability, "Eligible Receiver," PP&O HQMC; JCS Exercise, PP&O HQMC; MCSF Bn., PAC with HQMC IMADET, Washington DC; Operation Desert Shield/Storm HQ, 4th MCD,

Richmond, VA; N&M CIntelTrngCtr, Dam Neck, VA; Office of Naval Intelligence, Suitland, MD; DOD Security Institute, Richmond; DONCAF, WashDC; N&M CIntelTrngCtr, Dam Neck, VA, J2 Joint Reserve Unit, DIA, The Pentagon, WashDC.

Current USMCR unit: HQMC Intel IMADET; J2 Joint Reserve Intell. Unit, Pentagon.

Education: BA (political science), 1971 and MS (adult education and community relations, 1973, both from City College of New York; Syracuse University, administration, 1976-79; several military courses at Richmond, Coronado and Quantico.

He has been employed at Medgar Evers College, City University of New York, 1978-79; National Institute of Education, WashDC, 1979-80; Maryland State Department of Education, staff specialist, youth and at-risks programs, 1981-present.

DANIEL M. WALSH III, Captain, born Nov. 29, 1941. Graduated Providence College in 1964, commissioned 2nd lieutenant and reported to Basic School, Class 2-65. Reported for duty with Lima Co., 3rd Bn., 1st Marines in Vietnam. Participated in Operation Utah and was wounded in action.

Returned to the States and served as guard officer at Marine Barracks, USN Base, Boston, MA and later as CO of HQ Co., H&S Bn., MCB, Camp Lejeune, NC. In August 1967, he received an honorable discharge as a captain.

Awards include the Bronze Star w/ Combat V, Purple Heart, Combat Action Ribbon, PUC, NDM, VSM w/star, VN Armed Forces Cross of Gallantry w/Gold Palm, VN Armed Forces Civil Action Medal w/Palm, VCM w/60 Device.

Capt. Walsh has held several political positions and also owns Walsh Insurance, an independent insurance brokerage firm and the Bordeaux Co., a commercial printing company.

He is married to the former Kateri Bennet and they have seven children: Daniel, Bennett, Christopher, Michael, Kateri, Mary Alicia and Laura.

Bennett is a captain on active duty at USMC Recruiting Station, Springfield, MA.

KENNETH J. WALTERS, Colonel, received direct USMCR commission February 1971. Served in a variety of staff billets including S-2, 1/14 and G-2A, 2nd MAB, and at MCAGCC, 29 Palms; between 1985-87 he was assigned to J3 USCINCPAC; 1988-90, dept. chief  of INFOSEC, CNO OP-09N, awarded Navy Commendation Medal. Recalled to active duty Operations Desert Shield/Storm as senior marine watch officer, Navy Operational Intel Center, Strategy/Targeting Department; 1991-93, warning officer, National Intelligence Officer-Warning, National Intelligence Council; 1993-94, special assistant to DACofS, Intel, HQMC; ADDI, Intel Production, J-2, Joint Staff, The Pentagon, 1994-96, awarded Defense Meritorious Service Medal; OIC, HQMC Intel IMA Det., May 1996-99, retiring in July 1999.

Including four years as a special agent with Naval Investigative Service, 1968-72, he retired from a civil service career as the field office chief, Industrial Security, Defense Investigative Service, Los Angeles, in 1988. He held several positions with Lockheeds' "Skunk Works," including program security manager for the F-117 and F-22 aircraft programs between 1988-93.

He completed reserve courses at Quantico (AWS and C&SC), Coronado (MCAGTF staff planning), Air Command and Staff College, National Security Management Seminar, National Defense University, and the National Senior Intelligence Officer course, Defense Intelligence College, DIA.

While on nearly two years ADSW at HQMC, Intel Division, he served as the Marine Corps representative to the Intelligence Panel of the 1997 Quadrennial Defense Review. He also served as the Marine Corps' action officer to Reserve Intel, General Officer Steering Committee (1996-98).

In January 1968, he received a BA degree majoring in East European history from California State University, Northridge.

He is currently conducting damage assessments for the Diplomatic Security Service, Department of State, in both Washington, DC and internationally.

RONALD JACK "DOG SPOT" WATTERS, Lieutenant Colonel, born June 14, 1952 in Grand Rapids, MI. Training: OCS, September-December 1975; TBS, January-July 1976.

Units served with: 1st Engineers, Truck Co.; 3rd Bn., 7th Marines, 1st MarDiv.; 4th Tank Bn., 3rd Civil Affairs group, 4th FSSG.

Memorable experiences and achievements include being civil affairs team leader during coup/contingency, Philippines, November-December 1989; recommended for Navy Commendation Medal by IMEF G-4 for host nation liaison during Desert Shield/Storm.

His awards include the Navy Commendation Medal, Navy Achievement Medal, Southwest Asia Service Medal w/three stars.

He has BS in political science and history from Grand Valley State University, Allendale, MI.

Currently he is a transportation dispatcher with the Atlanta Auto Auction.

He is married with two step-children.

LUANN DOBECCA WEEKS, Lieutenant Colonel, born March 4, 1953 in Bay City, TX. Training: MCRD, Parris Island, June 1978; Admin. School, Schools Co., PISC, August 1978; Disbursing Officers Course, Schools Co., MCB, Camp Lejeune, NC, June 1982; Adjutants Course, MCSSS, MCB, Camp Lejeune, August 1990.

Units served with: Battery C, 14th Marines, Waterloo, IA, USMCR; Service Co., Kansas City, MO, USMCR; MCRSC, Overland Park, KS, FTS; Co. B, HQ Bn., HQMC HH; Support Staff courses for Reserve PME, Camp Clark, 1997 and Camp Crowder, 1989-99.

Memorable experiences and achievements include working at Equal Opportunity Branch at HQMC as a liaison officer for Women's Issues in 1993-94; being camp commandant for Reserve PME, summers of 1998 and 1999 at Camp Crowder, MO.

His awards include the SMCR Medal w/star, Armed Forces Reserve Medal, Meritorious Unit Commendation w/star, National Defense Service Medal and Navy Commendation.

She is married to Joe J. Weeks, USMC (Ret), and they are farmers.

JAMES T. "JIM" WHIPP, Major, born Sept. 7, 1934 in Eaton, OH. Training: Quantico, VA, September 1956-September 1957.

Units served with: 7th Communications Bn., FMF; 1st Service Bn., 1st MarDiv.; MABS-46, MAG-46, MCR, 4th MAW. He received two Reserve Ribbons/Medals.

He is a retired credit manager. He and his wife, Lois, have one son, Robert, and one daughter, Cheryl.

ALEXANDER P. "AP" WHITE, Colonel, born March 30, 1932 in Chicago, IL. Training: Naval Air Training Command, 1954-55, Pensacola, FL; Naval Justice School, 1968, Newport, RI.

Units served with: HMR-161, HMR-363, HMM-763, HMM-776, MACG-48, H&HS-4, MCDEC RAV.

Memorable experiences and achievements include Operation Redwing, Pacific Proving Ground, 1956.

Awards received: Letters of Appreciation: Gen. Arthur Adams, USMC; Honorary Commander, Law Co., NTC Great Lakes, IL, 1996-97, Merit Award, USMCR Officers Assn.

Education: Northern Illinois University, BS in business admin., 1959; Chicago-Kent College of Law, juris doctor degree (cum laude), 1964; John Marshall Law School, LLM, 1976; DePaul University, MS in management, 1978; Naval Justice School, 1968, 1972, 1980; USMC Command and Staff College, 1975; Brookings Institute, Public Affairs Forum, 1975; National Defense Strategy Seminar, Defense Strategy University, 1978.

Member of USMCR Officers Assn., Marine Corps Assn., Marine Corps League, Reserve Officers Assn., Navy League, USN Institute, American Legion, VFW and Marine Corps Combat Correspondents.

As a civilian he was an attorney, 1962-86, and Circuit Court Judge of Cook County, state of Illinois, 1986-present.

He and his wife, Marilyn, have four children: Bradley, Christy, Laura and Julie.

THOMAS WILSON, CWO2, born March 29, 1968 in Fort Ord, CA. Training: December 1990-May 1991, among the 70 Marines from Tucson, AZ activated and deployed to Saudi Arabia during Desert Shield/Storm.

Units served include Delta Co., Infantry Training School, Camp Pendleton; 1st Bn., 24th Marines, Detroit MI; GSGII, II MEF, RAS MEESHOB, Saudi Arabia; Bulk Fuel Co. Alpha, 6th ESB, 4th FSSG, Tucson, AZ.

Memorable experiences and achievements include BA degree, human resources/personnel management, Park College, Parkville, MO. Current plt. commander, Bulk Fuel Co. "A", Tucson, AZ.

His military awards include the Armed Forces Reserve Medal (mobilized), Select Marine Corps Reserve Medal (three), Southwest Asia Service Medal (three), Kuwait Liberation Medal and Kuwait Campaign Medal.

He has been a Tucson Police Officer for five years and is in his second year of law school at the University of Arizona.

He and his wife, Sandy, have one daughter, Carly, and a son due in September.

WILLIAM D. "BILL" WINTERS, Colonel, born Jan. 25, 1942 in Wichita, KS. Training: July-December 1965, TBS; January 1966-July 1967, flight training.

Units served with: VMFA-251, VMFA-122, VMFA-451, MATCS-48 DET D;, FMFLANT, CINCLANT.

Memorable experiences and achievements include flying 19 missions in RVN. Malaria kept him out of country after 1968.

BS degree, Stanford, 1965; MBA, University of Washington, 1972.

His military awards include Air Medal and other campaign and commendation medals.

Currently, COO Medical Device Co.

He is married with seven children/step-children.

GUY L. WOMACK, Lieutenant Colonel, born Jan. 23, 1953 in Atlanta, GA. Training: OCS, Quantico, October-December 1980; TBS, Quantico, January-May 1981; AWS, Quantico, September 1986-June 1987.

Units served with: Co. I, 3/2, XO, Rifle Co.; 1-23, S-3, operations and training officer.

Memorable experiences and achievements include being deployed with battalion in support of Operations Desert Shield/Storm, 1991.

His military awards include the Navy Commendation Medal, 1986 and 1990 and Navy Achievement Medal, 1984. Other significant achievements: chief trial counsel at Legal Services Support Section, 2nd FSSG; prosecuted capital murder cases at Camp Lejeune, NC.

Currently he is an attorney in criminal defense and federal employment law.

He and his wife, Kathy, have one son, Geoff, and two daughters, Paige and Amy.

ROBERT G. WORKMAN, CWO4, born July 20, 1949 in Laurens, SC. He joined the USMC in 1968 and completed basic training at Parris island, ITR at Stone Bay and supply school at Montford Point. After active service he joined the 57th Rifle Co. in Greenville, SC. The company was redesigned Ammunition Co. where he progressed through staff sergeant and was selected WO in 1978, completing supply and ammunition officer schools and holding assignments of platoon commander, operations and training.

In 1990 he served as operations ammunition officer, assistant chief of staff G-3 with Direct Support Command during Desert Storm and was awarded the Navy Commendation Medal.

He retired in 1993 and is senior accounting manager with one of the largest engineering firms in the US and services in law enforcement as a state constable.

Married to Cheyenne for 30 years and has son, Shane (airborne, air assault Army blackhawk pilot) and daughter, Wendy (criminal justice graduate and deputy sheriff).

THOMAS E. WORKMAN JR., Colonel, San Diego, 1945; TBS, Quantico, VA, 1951-52, US Naval School or Justice, Newport, RI, 1952.

Units served with include HQ Bn., Training and Replacement Command, HQ Co. 2nd Inf. Training Regt., Camp Pendleton (1952), H&S Co. 5th Marines, Korea (1953), 7th 90mm Gun. Bn., USMCR, Los Angels, 1955-56, VTU (Law), 12-31, Los Angeles, 1958-76.

He had no ambition to become a lawyer when he was commissioned in the USMCR in 1951. After he graduated from Naval Justice School, however, all billets to which he was assigned were as a legal officer. His experience in military law sparked his interest in becoming a lawyer when he was released from active duty in 1954.

His awards include the Naval Unit Citation.

He is a retired partner, Pillsbury Madison & Sutro LLP, Los Angeles, CA.

Col. Workman is married with two children and two grandchildren.

JACK B. ZIMMERMANN, Colonel, a native of San Antonio, TX received his commission as a 2nd lieutenant upon graduation from the USNA in June 1964.

Training: Basic School, Artillery Officers Orientation Course; MS degree, Krannert Graduate School of Management, Purdue University, 1969-70; JD degree, School of Law, University of Texas, 1972-75; Naval Justice School, Newport, RI, 1975.

Units served with include Btry. G, 3rd Bn., 12th Marines; Co. C, 1st Bn., 4th Marines, RVN, 1965; Btry. W, 3rd Bn., 12th Marines, RVN, 1966.

Assigned in 1966 to joint service Defense Atomic Support Agency, Sandia Base, Albuquerque, NM; 1968, HQ Btry., 1st Bn., 13th Marines, RVN; Btry. K, 4th Bn., 12th Marines; Co. B, 1st Bn., 23rd Marines; 1975, chief defense counsel, Force Troops, Atlantic, Camp Lejeune; 1976, 2nd MarDiv. as chief prosecutor and military justice officer.

Served 1978-81, USMCR as XO, 1st Bn., 23rd Marines, including duty in Norway on Operation Teamwork - 80; March 1981-82, S-3 of MTU TX-5, Houston, TX; 1982-83, XO of HQ Detachment 6, 4th MarDiv.

Assumed command of the 1st Bn., 23rd Marines, 1983; promoted to colonel in 1985 and served with MTU TX-5, Houston, TX; 1986-88, staff judge advocate, 4th Marine Aircraft Wing, New Orleans, LA; 1988-89, deputy chief defense counsel in Washington DC; 1989-91, HQ Det-6, 4th MarDiv., Houston, TX; 1991-93, group inspector for the 4th Force Svc. Gp., Atlanta, GA; 1993 to retirement in 1994 as reserve general courtmartial trial judge, Navy-Marine Corps Trial Judiciary.

His awards include two Bronze Star Medals w/Combat V, Purple Heart Medal, Meritorious Service Medal, Joint Service Commendation Medal, Navy Commendation Medal w/Combat V, Combat Action Ribbon, Presidential Unit Citation, two Meritorious Unit Commendations, and many service awards.

He and his wife, the former Ilene Weinberger of San Antonio, TX, have been married for over 34 years. They have two children: Terri Jacobs, a captain of Marines who is currently assigned to a Reserve billet as a judge advocate in Washington DC and is practicing law in Houston, TX, and David Zimmermann, a former captain of Marines who is working as an operations support officer on the international space station for NASA in Houston, TX.

Col. Zimmermann is a board certified specialist in criminal law and has been involved in several highly publicized cases in recent years.

We stole the Eagle from the Air Force,

The Anchor from the Navy,

The Rope from the Army,

And on the seventh day

when God rested,

We overran His perimeter

and stole the Globe

And have been running the show ever since.

United States Marines

The Marines Prayer

Almighty Father, whose command is over all and whose love never fails, make me aware of thy presence and obedient to thy will. Keep me true to my best self, guarding me against dishonesty in purpose and deed and helping me to love so that I can face my fellow Marines, my loved ones and thee without shame or fear. Protect my family. Give me the will to do the work of a Marine and to accept my share of responsibilities with vigor and enthusiasm. Grant me the courage to be proficient in my daily performance. Keep me loyal and faithful to my superiors and to the duties my country and the Marine Corps have entrusted to me. Make me considerate of those committed to my leadership. Help me wear my uniform with dignity, and let it remind me daily of the traditions which I must uphold.

If I am inclined to doubt, steady my faith: If I am tempted, make me strong to resist: If I should miss the mark, give me the courage to try again.

Guide me with the light of truth and grant me the wisdom by which I may understand the answer to my prayer.

Amen

VMA 134, MCAS El Toro, CO LtCol Stuart F. Nelson, 1964.

Lieutenant Colonel James J. Campbell and Lance Corporal George Mattis of the 6th Communications Battalion, Bronx, New York present Ivy Jiminez, a victim of Cooleys Anemia with a donation of blood to be used for future blood transfusions necessary to combat this dreaded disease.

BUILDING A BRIDGE

INDEX

Editor's note: Entries appearing in the biography section do not appear in the index since they are in alphabetical order in that section

(Courtesy of Col. J.J. Campbell)

Printed in the USA
CPSIA information can be obtained
at www.ICGtesting.com
JSHW060056150824
68134JS00032B/2747